How to Meet the Moment

A Guide for Precarious Times

Evan B. Carr

Tetraktys Press

How to Meet the Moment
A Guide for Precarious Times

Tetraktys Press
tetraktys@evanbcarr.com

First Edition

ISBN 978-1-966704-00-3

Library of Congress Cataloging-in-Publication Data is available.

Publisher's Cataloging-in-Publication Data
Evan Carr
How to Meet the Moment: A Guide for Precarious Times/ by Evan B. Carr. -- First edition.
209 pages
ISBN 978-1-966704-00-3

    1. Social change--United States

    2. Environmental responsibility

    3. Human ecology--Social aspects

    4. Sustainable living

    5. Personal growth

Printed in the United States.

2024.

Dedicated to Sheridan and Gordon
who gave me life
and to our ancestors
from whom we came.

Contents

Acknowledging

Chris, a better friend and brother-on-the-path a man could not ask for. Thank you for co-evolving on this journey and for being a man of virtue and honor. Your direct and indirect influence on the journey contained within this book is one of the greatest joys of my life.

My beta readers, Bree, Kristin, Matt, and Paula, who tolerated early draft versions and gave their honest (and sometimes brutal) feedback – thank you!

The many people who supported me personally during the difficult backdrop of my life as this book was being written including Allie, Chris, Deva, Jamie, Jessica, John, Matthew, Matthew, Meaghan, Michael, Stephen, the EDL, PP, and Kalpuli communities, and anyone else I forgot. I am humbled by your ongoing compassion and care and vow to pay it forward.

Paula, this book would not exist without your indelible influence on my development and life journey. There is much in this book I would likely not have experienced without your presence in my life. I am forever grateful. May we continue to share Health in this life.

Jessica, I could fill thirty volumes this size and never fully capture who you are to me and how I've grown in the seconds, minutes, hours, days, months, and soon year(s) since our junction. I am forever changed by our short time together. The beauty and connection described in this book and which emerges from the cavernous depths of my own awakened heart, will forever, in some way, be for you.

The future, which is obviously worth it, otherwise this book would not exist. Thank you for the inspiration <3

Preface

I can feel the fear as I write this. How easily it is to slip into the dark place where all is lost. Where it's too late and this book and all my actions are trivial in the face of impending doom. Opening the newspaper is an exercise in cognitive dissonance. All the signs are there if you look. Natural disasters. Food shortages. Geopolitical maneuverings for resources. And the sacrosanct capitalist drive for profit and consumption.

I wish I didn't have to write this book. That all those who came before me had done the hard work instead of shirking their responsibility. I tell myself "maybe *they*, those ones in control, maybe they didn't know" seeking to be a compassionate person. Maybe they just couldn't see all the long-term outcomes of their actions. Maybe it was never foreseeable. Maybe it's only becoming clear now.

Now I stand, like many others, peering over the precipice of the sixth mass extinction. Reading the latest science and pundits, absorbing the counter-points, attempting to make sense of it all, and seeing the scribbles on the wall as potentially dangerous enough to spell true disaster for our species.

I walk through the stores of national retailers utterly astonished at the volume of items on the shelves and the complex global supply chains that are required to bring these items to a random Walmart at a random stop along a highway in a state I'm only passing through. I see the headlines of fortunes made and lost in high finance through mergers and acquisitions — modern gladiator battles for prize and pride that seem so remarkably disconnected from the living, breathing ecology that provides life. I watch the symptoms of our dis-ease manifest as distraction and trivial pursuit while our true deeper human needs go unmet.

I wonder where the elders are, or even the adults for that matter. Why are they not the ones in control? And would that even change anything? Is it individuals or systems that need change? Who is really to say? How do I fashion my one wild and precious life nestled in context to the global, national, and local happenings?

Amidst all of this, how do I know what is mine? For what am I responsible? What skills must I hone to face the stark realities of our modern world? Who must I become in order to take the next right action? How do I fashion a life worth living amidst the million voices vying for my attention?

I embark on writing this book having spent years preparing to be able to discern these answers. I am filled with questions and an unflinching desire to Meet the Moment. This book is my earnest effort at wayfinding and offering an onramp to the skills one must develop if we are to truly witness what's happening and do more than nothing about it.

My attempt in this book is not to be right. Rather it is to engage you in a genuine and honest examination of the hard truth, the skills required to do that, and to serve as a type of GPS for your personal beliefs and actions. I've attempted to write this in as much plain vernacular as possible and to not overwhelm you with facts, figures, and anecdotes. It is my expectation that you will do background research to enrich your own reading of this book.

Before getting my masters degree my bachelor's degree was in interdisciplinary studies. This degree choice allowed me to study a wide variety of topics which is how I'm wired. I've never stopped studying and learning on a broad array of topics. I've taken many classes in a litany of different fields. Most importantly, I have invested 15 years, the entirety of my adult life, in a deep journey of inner work and personal transformation. This journey has led me to foreign landscapes to sit on the ground at the feet of elders and wisdom keepers. I've taken a multitude of courses and my bookshelf is overflowing. I believe strongly that in order to Meet the Moment we cannot rely on one type of knowledge, scientific and rational, over another, somatic and intuitive. We will only thrive if we have the space within ourselves to hold both in our faculties. This book is infused with spiritual principles from every tradition because spirituality is an essential key to meeting our moment, though perhaps not in the ways you might assume.

In many ways I think there's nothing spectacular about my personal experience that warrants such attention. My life has almost exclusively been insulated from adversity, bias, and issues of environmental or civil justice. I have neither lost loved ones or houses to natural disasters or felt any acute discernible impacts from our changing climate. In the scheme of things I have been an economic winner. And yet I can no longer look away from the uneven distribution of risk and crisis that permeates our world. That you might have felt the effects of our many crises likely only validates many of the inquiries in this book in a way that will "land much deeper in your body" in the wisdom gained from your actually-lived challenges.

In writing this book I have also kept in the corner of my eye that "Meeting the Moment" applies to more than just our moment. How might this have been relevant to people in World War II, during the Covid pandemic, or in the future when hostile aliens invade or civilizational collapse actually happens? The skills and capabilities discussed in this book should be relevant for many decades ahead. As an onramp into the many opportunities for deeper understanding, and more importantly, to develop personal and communal practice, I have included visible recommendations for further reading, quotes, practices, and prompts to journal on throughout the book

Threading the needle between objective facts and my personal experience while writing something that still feels alive and connected to that which is greater and deeper than me, you, or this book is a challenge only you can assess the degree to which I've been successful.

I assume that if you're reading this that something in your world, in your direct experience, has called you to a similar observation as me: that things seem to be falling apart, that the cracks are showing and have been for a while. What you've observed in your community, what you've felt in your place, the links you've clicked and the news you've watched, or the loss you've grieved, that within the depth of your livingness is a recognition that something just doesn't feel right and we as a society and a species are not trending in the "right" direction.

This sentiment is neither pleasant or comfortable and is a shallow preview of what we'll consider in the pages that follow. My promise to you is the same as it is to myself. I've written this book because I am choosing that even while holding all the doom and gloom, beyond death, destruction, and even hope, that there are ways to orient ourselves to Meeting the Moment in a manner that deepens our humanity, our capacity for care and connection, and increases our capabilities, readiness, and resilience.

It is my sincerest hope that I accomplish this task enough that you find some new place from which to engage in the conversation about our delicate moment in time. And while many of my own conclusions are shared in this book, what is ultimately more important to me is that you took the time and space to honestly consider the conversation. Your conclusions, and thus your actions, will likely differ from mine. If you feel more equipped to Meet the Moment then each of our time has been well invested.

I thought this book was about climate change when I started. But through writing it I realized that it has less to do with the realities of a warming planet and more with the underlying lifestyles and economic system driving it. I wrote this book because every book I've read on climate, and there are many good ones, is full of scholastic, scientific, and social solutions. Yet most fall short of truly addressing the processes for *how* one comes to make the internal shifts necessary to outwardly enact the systemic solutions called for or even just to personally adapt to what's coming before it occurs.

I do not claim to do everything in this book. I've done and continue the internal work. Writing this book has for me been a clarification of my beliefs as they are today which has exposed the gap between what I value and how my physical life is actually arranged. I've come to believe in the concept "don't believe what I say, watch what I do". And so in this way writing this book is a big risk in that it publicly and on-the-record opens me up to the criticism of being a hypocrite, of saying one thing and doing another, *if* I do not actualize many of the outward doing-oriented conclusions that are the results of the inner journey this book is really about.

I'll offer a warning, one similar to what was shared with me and one that I have found to be excruciatingly true: there is no going back. There is a point of no return which after you've crossed cannot be undone. It is simultaneously wonderful and full of clarity while being earth-shattering and challenging at the same time. Whether this book will be that for you depends more on your journey and personal readiness than on my writing.

To really "break through" most times you have to first break down. And to do that you have to understand something beyond just the intellectual level. You must feel it in your body. It must stir your emotions. You must feel something deep inside of you rise and writhe in response. It requires that you engage from a place within yourself that includes and yet is beyond the mind. Only then will you really "get it".

That's assuming "getting it" is even worth it to begin with. More knowledge does not explicitly lead to more peace or satisfaction. In an ideal culture there'd be nothing to learn and this book would be unnecessary. We would already get it having been raised in a manner that guides our living to be in right relationship with our ecological, human, and more-than-human worlds.

Embarking on this type of journey now, presumably as a Western adult without a deep ecologically-aware upbringing, is a process that likely requires months or years and for the truly initiated never ends. Besides an absence of elders, our culture has lost many of the hallmarks of one that helps its people actually get it. And so much like our quick-fix culture this book is actually an attempt to push the medicine quickly, to plunge the syringe rapidly, perhaps violently, into your intravenous line in hopes of flooding out, for a brief moment, all the other medicines (but more likely toxins) capturing your attention. I wish it could be a different way. But I don't think so. And I suspect we don't have the time. But let's not get ahead of ourselves.

My wish is that you read this book with all of your senses. Read with your heart. Listen with your body. Allow your imagination to wander into dark and scary places. Allow yourself to be riled up. Enter the fuzzy zone of unknowingness. Question long-held beliefs and discover you're still safe afterwards. Or maybe not.

Put yourself on the line. Place something dear on the altar. Dare sacrifice. Start broaching the conversation. Find the courage to trust your intuition. Rely on your knowing rather than someone else's agenda. Our future is worth it.

September 23, 2023
Evan B. Carr

Introduction

Meeting the Moment

We're embarking on a journey to Meet the Moment. This is the process of picking our heads up from the busyness of our daily life to take a deep and sobering look at what's really occurring in the world around us. It is about building perspective of how all this came to be, what's happening and why, and who we have to become to do something about it. It is the task of our times, our evolutionary call to develop our individual and collective capacities to live up to the responsibility of our modern power and progress.

Meeting the Moment requires courage and an array of other skills that enable us to hold the many feelings and thoughts that arise when trading our rose-colored glasses for the inconvenient truth. It is as much about Meeting the Moment within ourselves as it is about the world outside of us.

The Journey Ahead

Who is this book for? It is for those who have seen and felt the rickety foundation holding up our modern world. For those disaffected by the giant cogs of progress. For those left behind by a system of exploitation and greed. For those who've thrived in that same system but deep down in the innermost recesses of their heart feel that something is off. This is a book for truth seekers, change makers, community members, parents, and anyone who is even moderately interested in life continuing to thrive for many generations to come.

This book is not for people who already grasp tightly to their made-up mind. If you're not open to new perspectives, return this book to your book seller and continue on your merry way. It is possible there are many foreign, even objectionable, topics in this book.

If the mere exposure to or consumption of ideas counter to your own is a problem, don't bother. And yet that's the exact reason to go on this journey in the first place. This book is not for people who have no desire to wrestle with paradoxes, hold multiple truths, and expand their abilities and even their very being into new ways of knowing.

The structure of this book is laid out in three parts. In Part One, Our Moment, we'll work to take a look at the world we find ourselves in, starting first with the surface cracks before covering some tools that enable us to deeply examine the hard truths about our modern society. We'll engage our sensemaking about economics and energy, consider counter points to climate change, and examine the implications of what appears to be true. Part One is not without its challenges. The content challenges many dominant narratives about our world. Seeing our moment is disconcerting, depressing even. But our examination of the moment is required if we are to set the stage for the journey to come. All of the responses, thoughts, and emotions that arise in the process are the fuel required for the internal work ahead.

Our main theory of change in this book is that in order for us to rise to the occasion of our complex and challenging word, we must first do the internal work at the level of our being. To that end, in Part Two, Reconnecting, we emerge from the stark realities of our world and dive into the rich internal resources available to us. We'll grapple with loss and grief, review nervous system regulation, consider language, myth, and prophecy, outline the developmental task of our time, consider our own enoughness, move beyond hope to choice, and address justice and equality. This section of the book only outlines what is a truly personal and miraculous journey of transformation that almost assuredly requires significant time and effort outside of these pages. If successful in this work, through devotion and further exploration of the developmental practices contained within, Part Two illuminates a pathway to reestablishing a deep, mythopoetic connection to our places and some of the skills necessary to do so.

Having "done the work", Part Three, Coming Together, calls us back out into the world and to our future. We'll look at principles and models for operating effectively, uncover the rich tapestry of Place, and discuss many of the actions we can take to externally shape our personal worlds. If Part One sets the stage and context and Part Two sharpens our internal readiness, Part Three is where all of this work comes alive in our real everyday reality.

Our aim in this book is to process its contents on as many dimensions of our being as possible. This is not _only_ an intellectual pursuit. To that end, you'll encounter a variety of features that are meant to enrich your journey: Practices, Prompts, and Quotes are all laying on the page like little lures inviting you to deeper exploration. Like the further reading resources they are not filler nor are they recommendations. They are strong suggestions, requirements even, in order to undergo the transformational journey you are actually already on.

Our destination is more than understanding. It is a shift in being, a new "come from", a worldview that has been lost amidst "progress" yet is the antidote to our modern malaise. Our eye in this book will always remain towards developing our abilities to see and understand the moment and to develop ourselves into true adults, one's in relation to something greater than ourselves and ready to be of service even when that means doing hard things. Against the backdrop of an uncertain-and-likely-far-more-challenging future we must develop our internal faculties if we are to cope, adapt, and even thrive.

Part One: Our Moment

How do we decipher what our moment is? What are the signs that we've been sensing for many years that might inform us? What is the "polycrisis"? What skills and capabilities do we need to develop to better answer these questions? Who do I have to become in order to look at what's uncomfortable or inconvenient about our world?

How did modernity come to be? What's really true about climate change? How is the conversation larger than just the weather? What is "ecological overshoot"? How might things change, or not? What are the implications of all the information we will consider? What are the reasons to doubt climate change? Can't technology save us?

In part one, we'll answer these questions to gain greater clarity about "our moment". If we are to act, we must first observe and orient ourselves to the environment we find ourselves in.

So let's get started where many things begin...childhood.

One

Conspiracy and Cracks

Good thing mom was already in bed. She never would have let me watch the show. I must have been about six years old. It was the first time I ever saw a crack.

I came down to the tiled kitchen around 11 p.m. because I couldn't sleep. My father was still up, I imagine decompressing from one of his out-of-state work trips as a salesman in the aviation industry. He busily filled in his New York Times crossword puzzle and warmly welcomed my unusual intrusion into his routine. On the island counter was a tiny television, one of those four-inch battery-powered tabletop antenna devices. I was instantly pulled in by the investigative reporting and ominous background music. According to the man on the screen there was a second shooter on the Grassy Knoll. A cover up. A conspiracy! All was not as it seemed. My mind began to search for inconsistencies and unexplained mysteries.

As a child I prided myself on my collection of books on Unidentified Flying Objects and Egyptology, both topics that begged curiosity to look beneath the surface. What were these saucer-shaped crafts really doing? Why was their presence so well documented and pervasive all over the world? What was the real purpose of the Great Pyramid? What technology did they use to build it? There was more than meets the eye.

By the time I was a teenager these influences had me searching for the cracks in the dominant narrative. I went down the conspiracy rabbit hole. The internet was a glorious place when it's so new that your parents and teachers have no idea how to regulate its use. Soon I found myself researching about the Bilderberg Group and Trilateral Commission, organizations mythically famed as dark evil cabals intent on ruling the world for profit and domination. Conspiracies about population and mind control, weather modification, and alien technology all raced through my awareness.

The seeds of doubt were planted in my mind. But even then, I had trouble fully taking the bait. These ideas seemed plausible, certainly possible in an adolescent's imagination, but how could I be so sure? Who could be trusted? If I asked an authority figure, they'd dismiss it. They probably didn't know or hadn't done the research. On the other hand, trusting a Geocities site from the actual dawn of the internet written by a guy named Marvin from Maine seemed a bit sketchy too. How could one really know?

Then the Twin Towers came down on September 11, 2001. I remember exactly where I was, coincidentally off from school that day huddled around the television watching the terror unfold on live television with the sense that this was paradigm shifting but not yet knowing how. Do you remember? Take a second and go back to that moment when you first found out. Close your eyes. Breathe. Who told you? What was your reaction? How did it feel in your body? Did you watch the news? These moments are singed into our collective psyche, just like the Challenger Explosion, DDay, or COVID-19.

Some time later rumors began circulating that 9/11 was an inside job. The documentary *Fahrenheit 9/11* exposed "the truth". Building 6 fell without being hit. Explosive residue found on structural support beams. The Saudi cover up. It was all laid out for us. Another crack in the narrative. But who was really to know? How could us peons far from the seats of power and intrigue know with any certainty?

The challenge with conspiracy theories lies in one's threshold for believing in the validity of the theory it purports. It's called a theory, not a fact, for a reason. Since 100% confidence is unlikely, at what point do you assess that the theory has enough evidence to warrant merit or even belief? How credible are the information sources? What's their agenda? And what of your personal beliefs? How much do you want it to be true? How does it fit within your existing schema?

There are always alternative narratives. The challenge is when they depart from what is readily observable and enter the realm of imagination and fantasy without reasonable and concrete proof. Understanding where subjectivity and the relativity of one's perception ends and objectivity begins is an extremely difficult, perhaps impossible, task.

Yet we are left to look out into the world and make sense of it. Peddling in conspiracy theories can be dangerous. They abound over vaccines, celebrities, and climate change, etc...the list goes on. People hunger for narratives that expose "the truth" and address the gnawing instinct that something just doesn't feel right.

The best litmus test for conspiracy theories is: does it serve you? What's the utility of believing a certain theory over the mainstream narrative? How do you live into it?

What does it do to your emotional state? What actions does it drive? I hold conspiracy theories lightly now. Believing in one or the other has little utility for how I actually live my day-to-day life. They are usually on a scale I have zero influence over and typically don't make me into a better person. It's much more practical to examine what's in plain sight than to read the tea leaves for hidden breadcrumbs. What did come of my youthful indulgences into conspiracy-land was an aptitude for listening and watching for the cracks between the dominant narrative and observable reality.

Break Your Mother's Back

The cracks are all around us. They are easy to see on the surface. What's a crack? A crack is an observation about our world that something isn't quite right. It's the gap between the way it should be, or could be, and what actually is.

Cracks are what we lament. They're the things we dream we'd change if we had all the power and were left to our benevolent whims. Cracks are the obvious injustices in our world, the systemic imbalances, the "rigged system" that most people can get fired up about if they're in the right mood. If you're looking, the cracks are everywhere. They're impossible to ignore.

Cracks are the result of choices made by people who prioritized their own agenda, whether profit or ideology, over what's good for the most. It is the same zero-sum game of winners and losers that has dominated human history. They are the constraints that limit our greatest human potential and the systems that shape our policies, laws, processes, and beliefs. Cracks are limitations based on fear of change or fear of the other. They are the scarcity mindsets that drive competition. They are the hubris that places individual desires above collective health.

The impacts manifest in a myriad of symptoms; cracks that are easily visible from the surface. There are more cracks than we have the time or space here to observe. As the scale and scope of society continues to expand, the cracks multiply and become more obvious because they originate from deeper, more foundational issues. To Meet the Moment we must first discern what is actually true about it. To do so, we'll start with the surface cracks before going deeper.

The **economic cracks** show themselves most readily through our system of unfettered free market capitalism. As economics dominates our world, wealth inequality surges and tax policy is captured to ensure tax breaks, loopholes, and smoke-and-mirrors accounting benefit the rich who capture huge wealth instead of returning enough of the spoils back to the society which created it. Corporations operate with impunity, skirting or flagrantly breaking laws, prioritizing profits over well-being while receiving subsidies to further pad margins.

Around the world debt has become the new whip of slavery, created out of thin air and readily doled out in generous proportion to ensure the economic hamsters stay dutifully turning the wheels of economic consumption, dividends, and share buybacks. During the COVID-19 pandemic we printed unfathomable sums of money that will drive inflation and continue to prop up the financial house of cards, just as we did from the smoldering ashes of the 2007 financial crisis and housing collapse. It was a house of cards then as it is now. Tax revenues, even at record levels, do not cover the necessary investments we need in infrastructure, health, and education. Our infrastructure gets a failing or barely passing grade and if you ever questioned U.S. priorities consider that military spending is 11% of GDP and education spending is just 4%. Meanwhile housing affordability remains a major problem as the middle-class is squeezed. A million dollars isn't what it used to be.

The economic realities are tightly interlaced with the **political cracks.** Polarization is reaching fever pitch. The right quickly labels the responsibility of creating a healthy, functioning, and just society "socialism" and instead argues for the privatization of public goods and services and the goodness of people's hearts to take care of the gaps (which never actually happens).

The left attributes societal problems to systemic inequality and corporate greed, advocating for extensive government intervention and redistribution of wealth as solutions, which often results in "big government" and wasteful spending. Under each party we get the same process, financial rewards for the current majority but fail to effectively get the real change on the ground that meaningfully and significantly improves quality of life to the levels that are truly possible without the leeches first sucking out their share. You no doubt see your own sets of cracks in our political system, perhaps in relation to our two-party system, campaign finance, lobbyists, money and corruption, etc...?

The **social cracks** are connected with all of this. We are witnessing a breakdown of social cohesion. Issues of education, mental health, employment, and public services all intersect to make health, in all of its definitions, more difficult to attain. Technology exacerbates the breakdown in our social connection. We pin, snap, scroll, post, like, and mention, increasingly allowing our real life to be dictated by the digital. We've entered a "post-truth" era where every ingroup has its own narrative of reality and agreement on basic facts is hard to come by.

We've grown weak as a people. We're soft, with our two-day shipping and pampered lifestyles. We've ventured to control every aspect of our lives with greater precision, inventing a tool, app, or service for everything. So much of this is unnecessary, and yet how often do you get frustrated when two-day shipping takes four days, Netflix doesn't load the show you want, a website service gives an error, or Siri hears you wrong? As a people we've lost the resilience that was once the hallmark of our ancestors and have traded it for convenience and ease.

PROMPTS are important questions to consider. Sit with them. Ponder them. Discuss them. Journal them. Questions are the doorway to deeper understanding.

> **Prompt:** Each of us has our own unique purview on the many cracks that permeate the world we're enmeshed in. My list above is certainly different from your observations over time. Take some time to reflect on the cracks you've seen through your own observation and life experience. Make a list of the cracks you've seen yourself.

This exhausting list of cracks is far from complete. Each of these cracks and many, many more not mentioned is a small sign pointing towards the precarity of our global moment. They create tremendous pressure on the tired masses, our populace who are feeling the big squeeze on not just our ability to live well now, but perpetually into the future. Just like a crack in the wall of a house they emerge from issues with the structural foundation of our modern global home. And we must look even deeper if we are to truly understand our moment.

Two

Our Moment

The Polycrisis, Overshoot, and Risk

A ll of the many cracks, mentioned and not, emerge from a deeper crisis, a tremendously complicated web of intersecting domains that do not stand alone. Rather they interweave with each other creating a gordian knot that many refer to as the polycrisis. The polycrisis is a cluster of disparate crises and shocks that interact, entangle, and mutually reinforce one another. It is the nature of our globalized world of expanding connections that ensures each crisis in a multitude of ways intersects with several others. This makes it difficult to understand the best leverage points to get traction, leading to many of our global challenges feeling intractable because to attempt to solve one is to attempt to solve them all.

We are in the polycrisis, a moment when various crises interact in complex ways that are difficult to solve.

Taken together all of these cracks are symptoms of an unhealthy system that is fraught with enormous risk for our collective future. So far the modern structural foundation has not undergone a critical failure because there are enormous forces propping it up. But as we continue to race into the future we are loading more and more pressure onto the supports of our natural and man-made systems. As population and commerce increase we are increasing the likelihood that one or more catastrophic events will simultaneously occur that significantly impact human civilization on a global scale. These existential risks (x-risks) are both man-made and natural, occurring through complex sets of interactions few if any can fully understand. Among the man-made x-risks are artificial intelligence, synthetic biology, nuclear war, nanotechnology, global system collapse, and inaction. The natural x-risks include super volcano, asteroid impact, and solar flare. And a few x-risks sit right at the intersection of human activity and natural forces: global pandemic, ecological catastrophe, and extreme climate change.

Each risk is substantially more complex than a simple sentence can describe. There is incredible depth and nuance in each of these domains and the many policies, people, and organizations that engage with them. There are experts in each of these fields who are dedicating their time, attention, and money to improving these dynamics. Their immense efforts are a testament to the power of the systems of extraction, profit, and control that fashion a resilient status quo standing against the needed changes.

Since 2020 we've witnessed a pandemic, supply chain disruptions, open wars in Europe and the Middle East, extreme temperatures and escalating climate issues, information warfare, biodiversity loss, and the acceleration of artificial intelligence. It's safe to say the frequency of existential risk is increasing.

The Courage to See and Feel

Stop. Take a moment to breathe. This is a lot. Close your eyes. Check your gut. How real do these existential risks seem to you? How do you feel in your body? Expansive? Contracted? What emotions come up for you?

Wait. Stop. Did you just read the previous paragraph and not do it? That's what I often do. Or promise myself I'll do it later. If so, this is exactly how you won't "get it". It will stay as the object of your intellect rather than a felt experience. If you're not willing to engage in this manner, better to stop now, put the book down, and not waste your time. This book is not only an intellectual pursuit. We must endeavor to experience the observable world through multiple ways of knowing. What happens inside of you when you venture to really hold everything already mentioned? Take a moment and *sit with it*.

The act of witnessing is one of the most beautiful and sacred activities we can engage in. In Indigenous cultures, the most powerful healers are the shaman, a word literally meaning "the one who sees". In the vedic tradition one of the most powerful blessings that you may have heard at your yoga class is Namaste, "the light within me recognizes the light within you".

Developing the ability to see, particularly in a manner that allows us to maintain neutrality, is essential on the developmental path towards being able to Meet the Moment. And we must not look away from the cracks and risks. That doesn't mean these realities won't bring up emotion. I can easily find my anger, blame, disappointment, frustration, hope, care, and connection when I hold the panoply of cracks in view. Can you? Creating the space for these responses is an essential part of the process and must not be short-changed.

The Individual and the System

It's easy to move quickly towards blame, anger, and frustration after briefly reviewing the cracks and risks of our world. It's THEM. It's THEY. The ones in control. And of course on the simplest level it's true. A privileged few sit above the fray making decisions and reaping the rewards while others pay the price of the externalities that are pushed off their books onto the commons and the people attached to them.

It's easy to read the news and see the many decisions that alienate life. Let's create a fictional CEO, Tom, a highly-educated MBA with a pedigree of privilege. Tom, like many of his peers, is willing to choose profit over the environment and people. He has learned to optimize decisions that maximize revenue at the expense of his social and ecological responsibility and to be rewarded handsomely for it. He donates some money on the back end to a nonprofit or two and tells himself it all evens out. And he even instructed his company to create an ESG department and makes some incremental changes that are on-trend according to his marketing advisors.

How does Tom come to make the decisions that denigrate our life-support system and the people attached to it? It's simple: Tom is disconnected. His connection to that which sustains life has been lost, replaced by the immediacy of consumer goods and his presumption of superiority, a twisted form of economic Darwinism that rewards his "superior decision making".

One does not simply lose their connection to life by accident. If it was one person perhaps it'd be something quirky and maladaptive about their character. But disconnection from life is a fundamental characteristic of Western society that has only increased as industrialization and urbanization has expanded. Our tendency to prefer logic over emotion has allowed us to break the world down into smaller and smaller parts, to mechanize how it all works into models, theories, and processes while dismissing the unknowable, unnameable, ineffable miracle of life that lies behind the curtain of certain human understanding. Perhaps you prefer to call this force God, or Spirit, One, the All, Tao, the Godhead, or the name of your preferred deity. It's the same "first mover" that all of the greatest physicists came to admit must exist which we've worked to distance ourselves from in our pursuit of secularism.

The more developed and technologically-enabled your place of living, the farther you are, on average, from the daily inputs that actually sustain life. Not Starbucks, shopping runs to the mall, and full aisles in supermarkets. The living breathing humming buzzing gnawing thrashing mooing neighing trickling chopping digging flying swimming growing and dying that takes place "out there" beyond the neatly organized city-gridded streets, reliable power sockets, and on-demand there's-an-app-and-billionaire-founder-for-that everything.

Back to Tom, our imaginary CEO. Do we blame Tom? Is he individually responsible for the decision to expand the oil pipeline through pristine wilderness or burying a known manufacturers defect that costs lives? Or is Tom the product of his environment, a culture who arranged all of the factors perfectly so Tom doesn't feel connected to his empathy, compassion, emotion, and ultimately to the possibility of the depth of his own humanity and all of life? The answer is yes.

One of the most amazing qualities of the Homo Sapien is our sheer cognitive flexibility which allows us to wrestle with paradox and simultaneously hold opposites and have them both be true. Earlier I mentioned the concept of zero-sum, which said in another way, is either/or. Either I win or you do. Either I lose or you do. We are well programmed for this type of thinking because there are so many situations in life where this is the case. Either you missed your flight or you didn't. Either you got the job or someone else did.

But either/or thinking is not *always* suited for the topic at hand. And so when we consider blaming them, the easy route to take is: either they are the ones responsible, or not, and I need a scapegoat, a target of my disdain and ire, so *they* are guilty. It's their fault. Phew!

But the truth is not so simple. Is Tom responsible for his individual action? Yes. Do we let Tom off the hook for that? No. AND it's important to acknowledge the systemic factors that have created the environment which makes it easy, even encouraged, to make the choices he does.

The reality is that we live in a culture that idolizes financial success and creates all the incentives to get it by just about any means possible. And the laws and enforcement are designed in a way where corporations have plenty of latitude for questionable behavior while rewarding shareholders, and of course, the "leaders" whose personal compensation and bonus packages increase, environment and people be damned. The CEO didn't design this system themselves. It's the result of a long slow campaign that no one person orchestrated. It creeps over time and little by little the bar of acceptability gets lowered until the norm becomes the cracks we lament.

The uncomfortable reality is that our corporations and institutions are hydras. The hydra is a mythical multi-headed dragon beast who when loses one head grows back two. The term is often used to describe drug or terror organizations for their ability to proliferate over time. This is because of a basic universal law: nature abhors a vacuum. When a seat of power is vacated it takes very little time for it to be filled by a new custodian ready to reap the rewards. To the victor the spoils...until the next victor.

So we can blame that particular oil company CEO. And they do shoulder responsibility. But it's best not to kid ourselves. If it were not them, it would be someone else and so we must also be clear that it is the system itself that must be held to account. This is of course difficult to do because the system is not one person in particular and changes over time. Yet this systems-level change is the work of our time which we'll visit in later chapters.

All of this is to say: no one is in control. *They* are not out to get you. There's no grand conspiracy. And if there really is a dark evil cabal ruling the world it looks like they're pretty bad at their jobs. There's small conspiracies but not some broad overarching plot of world domination. The complexity of the polycrisis and the hydra-nature of positions of power ensure that no one is at the helm. Really sit with this. Consider that it's a lot more random than you might have previously assumed.

No one person is in control. There is no elite club of evil overlords gleefully creating this polycrisis. And the train is going off the tracks. Multiply the stuckness of our many crises times the expansion of population and economies and you'll get the incredible momentum at which we're rapidly approaching the edge. In the past when I pictured this train going off the tracks I always saw the scene as if I was an observer watching from a distance. Until it dawned on me *that I'm on the train along with everyone I've ever met.* There's no conductor. Instead each of us is an engineer, and to one degree or another, our begrudging or unwitting compliance with the systems-that-be ensures that each of us is, shovel in hand, tossing more coal into the engine.

Overshoot: The Mother of All Cracks

Herein lies the fundamental problem: coal. Or, fossil fuels to be exact. Despite the immensity of cracks previously mentioned, all of them are ultimately nested within the mother of all cracks: overshoot. Not climate change. Our rapidly changing climate is a symptom of the disease our planet is now riddled with called ecological overshoot. Overshoot is defined by a few well-documented characteristics which can be readily observed including exceeding the **carrying capacity** of the planet as growing populations all strive for first world standards of living and thus leading to **resource depletion** at a rate far more quickly than can be regenerated by the planet in the time scale of its natural processes. It is driven by the unwavering belief of infinite growth on a finite planet. It is a crisis which threatens to swallow every other. Overshoot is bringing us closer and closer to the edge.

What good is a functioning education system if all the schools have burned down? What good is a more equitable economic system if we've depleted our resources? What good is a more just society if the masses of humans are hot and hungry? If we have a planet that is not conducive to human living then all else is a moot point. As many have noted our planet will be fine because it is working on geological time scales. Human civilization, however, is a cosmic blip on this time scale and could easily disappear.

Based on complex and earth systems science, researchers at the Stockholm Resilience Centre have identified nine planetary processes that regulate the Earth's stability and the boundaries for each beyond which significant, potentially irreversible changes to our planet's functioning may occur. The nine planetary processes that are essential for us maintaining a habitable planet are climate change, biosphere integrity (biodiversity), modification of biochemical flows (the nitrogen and phosphorus cycles), introduction of novel entities (synthetic chemicals, metals, and plastics), land system change, freshwater change, stratospheric ozone depletion, ocean acidification, and increases in atmospheric aerosols (tiny particles in the air). In 2018, the second version of the model assessed that four of the nine planetary boundaries had been crossed. As of 2024, the third version of this model now shows that six of the nine planetary boundaries are beyond the safe threshold for human life. The longer this occurs the more likely we are to cross a tipping point, a threshold of no return where fundamental geophysical functions break down.

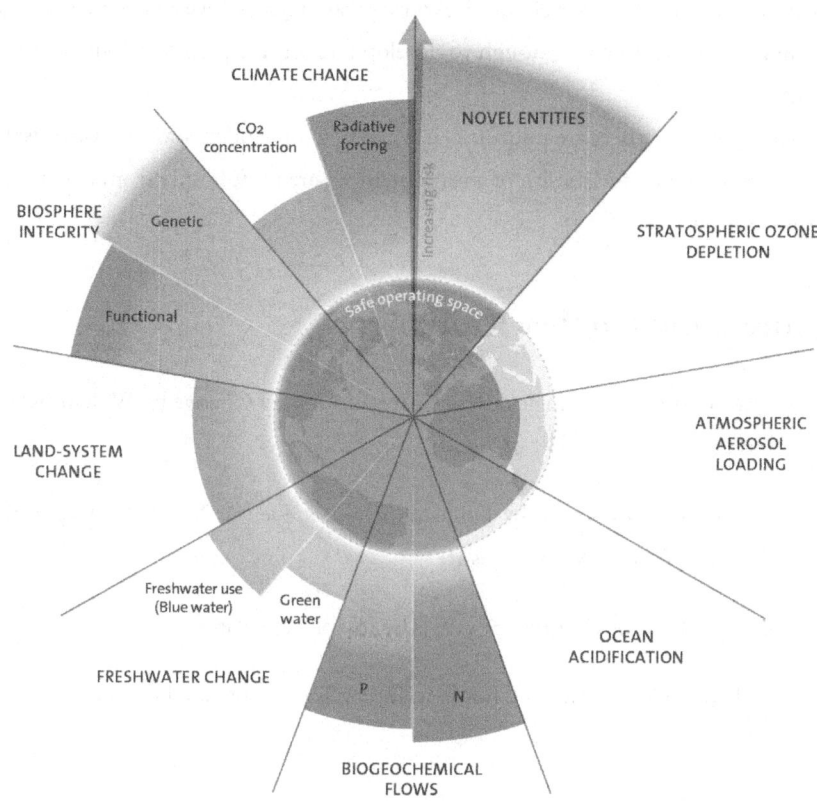

CLIMATE CHANGE

CO₂ concentration

Radiative forcing

NOVEL ENTITIES

BIOSPHERE INTEGRITY

Genetic

STRATOSPHERIC OZONE DEPLETION

Functional

Safe operating space

LAND-SYSTEM CHANGE

ATMOSPHERIC AEROSOL LOADING

Freshwater use (Blue water)

Green water

FRESHWATER CHANGE

P

N

OCEAN ACIDIFICATION

BIOGEOCHEMICAL FLOWS

Credit: Azote for Stockholm Resilience Centre, based on analysis in Richardson et al 2023.

We will invest our attention in a brief summary of the latest climate science later in Part One, though it's important to keep in mind that the changing climate is only one element of the broader reality of overshoot. Our purpose in this book is not to prove that human-accelerated climate change is real. There are plenty of full-length books about what's happening to the climate for you to read, or you could just look out the window and make an informed assessment.

The hot take (literally) is that the climate looks bad and is trending worse. As our weather swings to greater extremes our food, infrastructure, and human losses suggest we will never have the opportunity to address the social, economic, or cultural crises. Which is of course ironic, and the quintessential nature of chicken or the egg, because it is our many other crises that hinder our ability to address overshoot in the first place.

The previous pages are a summary attempt to paint a superficial picture of what's happening by examining cracks, existential risks, and overshoot. But if we are to Meet the Moment we must have an even deeper understanding of what's happening. Meeting the

Moment requires that we uplevel ourselves with great urgency if we are to rise to the task of opening our aperture wide enough to develop an accurate picture of our precarious moment.

To assure you now, there are solutions - it is not all doom and gloom. But we must first start with an honest consideration of the moment we are in. It is only from here that we can begin to grow.

Resources and Further Reading

- Overshoot: The Ecological Basis of Revolutionary Change by William R. Catton Jr.

- The Limits to Growth by Donella Meadows, Dennis Meadows, Jørgen Randers, and William W. Behrens III

- The Collapse of Complex Societies by Joseph A. Tainter

- Collapse: How Societies Choose to Fail or Succeed by Jared Diamond

Three

Theory of Change

The developmental path to effectively addressing the seriousness of our collective situation requires a variety of skills. We must develop the internal capacities that empower us to not look away from a reality that is unpleasant and often too much to handle if the depths of our humanity is to be shaken.

A theory of change is a model of how growth and development occurs. It models how a specific set of strategies and actions lead to certain outcomes. Theories of change are important to identify because they require us to have a working model of how we as individuals, organizations, and societies will grow.

Our Theory of Change: To Meet the Moment, we must do the internal work before taking external action.

Put simply, being before doing. How does this feel intuitively? True? And yet how often do we gravitate towards doing first? We assume that more action will solve the problem. If we build it they will come. We invest our time, attention, and money bringing a solution to reality only to see low adoption or a set of unintended consequences that must then be addressed. Our cultural bias for action ensures that there is always plenty to do yet we often skip the essential step of first finding clarity within our being. This "being" level is our home base, our "come from", the place within ourselves from which all else emerges. Within our being is nestled our personal beliefs, thoughts, emotions, fears, senses, and relationships. They are the *why behind the what.*

Another way to tease out this theory of change is to say that power is upstream. Our results, actions, and decisions are shaped by what's upstream: our feelings, beliefs, and experiences. The principle of PEMDAS we learned in early math class taught an enormously important lesson: that the order of operations matters. As with the world outside of us, internally there is an order of operations in how we arrive at our decisions and the actions that follow from them. This vast internal world full of feelings, beliefs, programming, associations, aversions, desires, and traumas is the "first mover". It sits at a higher order of power, upstream of doing at the level of our being.

The being-level work is essential because it is the place from which our resilience emerges when the going gets tough. With a clearly defined why we are able to source the wherewithal to sustain action over time. Meeting the Moment is tough, both internally within ourselves and externally in the world. It requires will. If we are ever to successfully effect broad personal and systemic change we must first evolve our state of being.

Put A Fork In It

To understand why we see individual or collective behaviors we must dive to the level of the being to understand the root cause. Let's look at the example of meat-eating. It is widely known that meat consumption within the modern diet is a significant driver of ecological damage. This is driven by mass deforestation to create grazing land, the emissions associated with raising animal feedstock, and the methane produced by cows. Estimates from the United Nations place the consumption of meat as contributing between 11% and 15% of total human greenhouse gas emissions from the 90 billion animals slaughtered each year. The science on how these emissions occur throughout the entire value stream of meat production is rigorous and robust.

And the solution is clear: reduce (or stop) eating meat. Today. Shift to a more plant-based diet or become a vegetarian and you will both immediately improve your health outcomes and reduce your carbon footprint. So how come more people don't reduce or eliminate their meat consumption? It's not particularly difficult when compared to many of the other behavioral changes suggested by taking immediate climate action like driving, flying, or buying less. It's literally just putting something different in one's mouth. All we have to do is buy something different from the store or order something different from the menu and put these veggies on our fork. Easy enough, right?

If the action is simple then there must be something going on at a deeper level, and there is, at the level of being. Once someone has heard the extent of ecological damage associated with meat-eating, and many have been exposed to this idea, there is some set of beliefs, emotions, and thoughts that keeps them from taking a different action. Being before doing. We don't have to unpack the many ideologies, resistances, entitlements, denials, fears, or preferences around meat consumption to see that our action emerges from beneath the surface.

Why is this important? Well the uncomfortable truth is that the moment requires us to make some challenging and inconvenient behavioral changes. If we, the collective we as a people, can't do the easiest thing of reducing meat consumption, how will we ever do the hard things? We won't. Not without doing the inner work first. I could have bludgeoned you with five times as many facts about meat consumption. Or written far more about the cracks and x-risks. Are more facts, figures, and science really going to move the needle in the conversation? No.

Science has its place in creating deeper understanding and we need more understanding about how our world works. But more science is not the answer to our problems. Addiction is the perfect example. We have a deep understanding about how hard drugs affect neurochemistry and destroy the body. There is ample evidence and huge efforts to get the information out about how dangerous substance abuse is. But does this stop addiction? The addicts know the science. They learned it from D.A.R.E, a treatment facility, therapy, or jail. And yet they continue their abuse. Science alone doesn't solve addiction because addiction is a psycho-spiritual phenomenon as much as a physical/chemical one. Dive deep enough and there is trauma, trapped emotion, and a lack of personal skills and communal or family support required to escape addiction. And much like substance addiction, modern society has its own set of addictions.

Our moment in time cannot be addressed through more science alone. It is a matter for our hearts and souls. Facts and figures will never land in a being whose heart is not open. More information will never register with someone whose soul is not connected to that which is greater than them. This is why any book that is serious about addressing the polycrisis or existential risks must also boldly open itself to personal development, and to the spiritual, numinous, and metaphysical. Our efforts here in this book must be rigorous if we are to Meet the Moment, and thus we must leave no stone unturned in seeking a depth of understanding and personal growth.

A Developmental Crisis

At the root of all the beauty at risk in the world is our developmental crisis. We have a culture that is inadequate in fully growing and maturing our people. As a result a *majority* of our population is stuck in a state of adolescence. Adolescents are focused on themselves and act as such. A true adult is a person who has matured to understand themselves as one in relation to a greater whole and how their unique, Creator-given role serves that whole. True adults are nurturing, generative, wise, connected to others, resourced for the challenging tasks at hand, and much more. They have come into their service and responsibility for *all* of life.

When one becomes a parent there are a certain set of decisions that are both immediately on and off the table. You will absolutely do some things and not others. There is no other way to love and responsibly take care of a child. Being a parent immediately shifts one's values and thus the decisions they are willing or not willing to make (we hope).

In the same way, reaching true adulthood brings an evolving set of values that are connected to something greater than oneself. True adulthood is not about taking on a temporary role, like a costume, job, or uniform, but discovering the role you were born for and how that shapes the nature of your relationship to the world, your community, place, people, family, and nature.

The answer to this developmental crisis cannot be purchased. One does not become an adult by having kids, a mortgage, or a car payment. One is not an adult by nature of their business accomplishments, the size of their bank account, and the esteem within which they're held. True adulthood is a developmental journey that opens up the capacities you were born with to intimately grow your connection to life.

Plenty of people emphasize viable point solutions to the polycrisis with the common phrase "We have the solutions. Implement them." Indeed we do. What's standing in the way of greater collective action is the personal economic incentive not to make change by those who have the power to do so. But what lies under that choice for each of those individuals, and for each of us in our own contributions to overshoot, is an adolescent culture devoid of its rightful and necessary connection with life. We are pointing out the problems and solutions until we're blue in the face. To move the needle en masse we must address the development crisis underpinning our inaction.

The great task of our time is the transformation we must each undergo. It is my quest, and your quest, for our hearts and souls, for if we can't individually claim the birthright of belonging our culture will never be able to either. Change is an inside job, first. And that takes time and effort. Just as a plumber needs the right tools for the task, each of us needs the right tools for our inner work.

Four

Tools for the task

There are many skills to cultivate on the developmental journey towards being a healthy, functioning adult. In this journey our work is never truly done. Individually and collectively we must work to realize our species' greatest potential. Many in our culture believe that technology is our greatest potential and herald the arrival of artificial intelligence, space travel, and quantum computing as proof. Our true greatest potential lies not in emerging advanced technologies but internally in our abilities to be healthy, communicative, mindful, and actualized.

Unfortunately "technology" has become ubiquitous with hardware like our cell phones and software like a computer runs. We forget that language is perhaps our most important technology as are the cognitive and psychological models that allow us to process personal events and feelings. The capacities each of us needs to develop to be able to witness and address the enormous challenges we face are types of technology. We will cover many different types of developmental tasks throughout this book enough to understand why it's worth it to invest your precious time enhancing your capabilities. A couple paragraphs or pages does not do them justice when compared to the large bodies of study and practice dedicated to each.

This chapter is the longest of the book for good reason. You might consider reading this section in multiple sittings. The following tools and developmental tasks are important in laying the foundation required for a deep and honest examination of our moment in the next chapter. To get the most out of this book, and life, it is strongly recommended that you invest significant time developing these and other related skills in an ongoing manner.

Self-Awareness

If there is one capacity to develop before any other it is self-awareness. What is it? Self-awareness is the ability to observe and reflect on what is occurring for you. Seems easy enough, right? I mean you can hear the voice in your head that makes up your thoughts so that's pretty much it, yes?

Not quite. The truth is that we are unfathomably complex creatures. Sure you can hear what you think, but *why* do you think it? What past experience or exposure to some person, belief, or idea is influencing your thoughts? What is the why behind the what?

We extend far beyond thinking. What are you feeling at this very moment? Is something arising while reading this? What emotions are in the background of that from your day, week, or overall period in life? Where does this emotion live in your body and what does that tell you? Is that important feedback? How well are you able to observe yourself from outside of yourself? Can you be an objective viewer of you? Can you critique your own actions and beliefs? Is your Self secure enough that change is possible when you uncover areas to metamorphosize?

All of this and much more lies within the realm of self-awareness. It is our ability to orient, track, and understand ourselves. Without high self-awareness we are as NPCs in a video game, nonplayer characters who are living life on automatic and executing our preprogrammed function without the ability for self-directed thought. Through self-awareness we understand what's really going on at ever deeper levels. So how does one develop self-awareness?

Ugh, not another recommendation to start a journaling practice. Lame! Except not. Journaling is one of the best methods to cultivate more self-awareness. It's the cheapest form of therapy. Your journal is a container that will listen to everything you have to say at any time. That's actually pretty great. And journaling provides you the ability to go back, read, and reflect on your own thoughts. Hot tip: start small. Set out to journal for a measly two minutes a day. Do this for a week. When the timer goes off, put the pen down. Notice if you start feeling like two minutes is not enough time. My journey to a daily journaling practice started much like this and the rewards have been truly tremendous.

While journaling, or after you've ignored the above recommendation because you don't have time or it's too tedious, watch for the stories you tell. Stories are one of the most common ways that we proliferate ideas that don't serve us yet we often don't recognize this because we're caught up in the story we tell. Recognize stories by turning a critical lens on your communication. When you are recounting something about your past, examine closely whether the way you choose to language past events is *actually* what happened. Or is it possibly your *interpretation* of what happened.

In grade school there's an art assignment and all the other kids *seem* to get more praise than you. Though it's not true, your interpretation is that "I'm not creative". You repeat this thought often enough over the years that by the time you're an adult you tell people your story: I'm not creative. What happens is that we project stories about our past into our future and soon they become self-fulfilling prophecies that don't actually serve us. Turns out you have decades of repressed creative energy and you're much more creative than the story you'd be telling. Surprising to no one but me, this was my story. Becoming aware of the stories we tell about ourselves and others is a useful method to increase self awareness.

With improved self-awareness we are able to more readily perceive the constant feedback our body, thoughts, and feelings are giving us. As you read this book it is essential that you observe what arises within you. What reactions occur when you read something challenging or objectionable? What is absent when you are prompted towards more connection? To make sense of this book, and our world, it is essential to peel back the surface layer of what presents itself to us and understand the deep causes of why we think and feel a certain way.

Sensemaking Skills

In the cloister of the lockdown, I along with many others dived into a set of cognitive skills defined as sensemaking. This set of skills became indispensable in making sense of the complexity of our world which became more evident to the naked eye through stressed supply chains, mandatory lockdowns, and drastic economic swings. Sensemaking is the ability to engage in non-biased assessment of the world and its dynamics and events. It includes:

- Improving self-awareness of cognitive biases and logical fallacies which are common errors in our thinking

- Increasing the ability to hold opposite ideas in mind at the same time, this is the capability to wrestle with paradox and expand understanding across the spectrum of a topic

- Challenging ourselves to see the holes in our own argument, the merits of someone else's, and engage in healthy dialogue

- Honing media literacy and growing the ability to acquire new and necessary information effectively

- Evolving from belief to perspective and establishing sovereignty of thought casting off the many agendas that seek to influence our thinking

- Deepening critical thinking and expanding one's purview into new domains and practicing systems thinking

The outcome of this work is a heightened ability to be able to see through propaganda and outside agendas instead piercing to the heart of the matter. Together this set of skills allows you to make sense of modern domains that are increasingly noisy and complex.

There's no shortage of information in this book. And there is incredible information available on every crisis. Sensemaking is an essential tool in addressing the immense ever-expanding scope of our world. It helps us to decipher how much we need to know in order to develop an informed perspective. Adopting a sensemaking lens is a constant practice of processing the shifting dynamics of the world that encourages us to be flexible, adaptable, and open to evolving our perspectives as new information becomes available. As you read further you must engage your sensemaking to determine the accuracy and applicability of the concepts ahead.

Context is Queen

Consider that everything is contextual. As in, what is true in one context might not be in another. Let's test this quickly. It's true that I'd never cut off my arm; unless it was pinned by a boulder and it was that or death. A firm handshake is a friendly or professional gesture; unless you're in Asia where it's considered rude. I'd never yell loudly in a movie theater; but if there is a fire I would.

Things can be true in one scenario but not in another. This is the basis of context. What is right for regenerating the ecological health of the Sonoran desert in the US Southwest is not what's appropriate for regenerating the burned Boreal forests of Canada. Their contexts are different. The same can be said for human relations, geopolitics, business deals, and most things.

Context is the environment in which our focus is nested in. What's occurring around our focus? What has changed or is changing? Who are the actors at play? Who has what agenda? What forces are at work? What are the limitations or constraints? These and many more considerations help us determine context.

Without understanding context it is difficult for us to effectively make sense of the world. Oftentimes we have to seek out more information so we "can get the full picture". Soon in Part One we'll dive deeper into the realities of our moment to place ourselves in context to what's occurring. This context will create the imperative for the journey of personal transformation we'll consider in Part Two as a response.

Ego

Much is made of ego in our world. What is ego? Ego is the Self we identify as, our mental construction of "me" as our body, thoughts, feelings, and actions, what we know as our identity and project externally to the world. In day-to-day terms you'll often hear someone refer to ego and mean the self-esteem or self-importance within which they hold themselves.

The goal of working with our ego is to ensure that it is healthy, but not domineering, humble, yet still effective. Modern society is full of adolescent ego spurred on by marketing, media, celebrity, and pop culture. Adolescent ego is self-centered whereas adult ego is life-centered. The journey of ego maturation moves from the adolescent altar of our own accolades to the soup line of soulcentric service. Carl Jung talks about this as the process of individuation where one casts off the photocopied veneer of culture-at-large and goes inward on a deep journey to 1) integrate the unconscious and our shadow, 2) encounter the masculine and feminine within us, 3) develop the true Self, and 4) reveal a personal myth, a narrative that gives meaning to one's life experiences (which we'll examine in Part Two).

Short of going on this substantial journey, which will inevitably involve forms of ego death if we are to be reborn healthier, working with ego is a wonderful direction to point our deepening self-awareness abilities. By seeking the internal motivations of our behaviors and thoughts we begin to peer into our subconscious and reveal the repressed ideas, weaknesses, desires, instincts, and shortcomings hiding in the darkness within. This is the essence of "shadow work", looking into the dark places within us to make the unknown known. It is the practice of "parts work", the growing body of therapeutic practices that understand our multi-faceted selves as collections of separate-yet-related parts. These parts are how we can have conflicting ideas or emotions within us and how it seems we have lived so many lives. Ego work includes our self-awareness of these parts, how they comprise our Self, and journaling or professional facilitation are both effective in exposing us to ourselves.

In the process of ego maturation, the trivial interests and personality traits we developed as adolescent strategies to find belonging outside of us fade away as we anchor our identity in the true inherent value we're born with and have now uncovered within; what many call Soul. This is dangerous for an economic system that needs you consumptively grasping outside yourself to define your worth. Ego that is rooted in the depths of Soul is humble rather than braggadocious, connected to life, and eager to be in service to others rather than self. As you read this book and engage with the world throughout the process, use your self-awareness to observe how the ideas may challenge your sense of identity. Notice how quickly you dismiss an idea. Usually the stronger and more vociferously we deny something, the stronger the defense mechanism in place that is seeking to keep some aspect of our ego safe. This is because our ego builds significant defenses to keep it from being destroyed, of course, it believes it is us. What you might discover is that "you" are perfectly safe without the large portions of your ego that were fashioned by external forces. That on the other side of any loss of ego is the potential of a more integrated and whole version of yourself. Releasing all of the ways we compensate to keep us safe while integrating all of the parts we repressed is no small task!

The journey in this book illuminates much of this work, particularly in Part Two, that evolves our ego into a more mature and connected state. In order to engage our best sensemaking about our moment, it is neccessary to have a loose grasp of our ego, to secure within ourselves that the goal isn't to be personally right, propping up our existing perspectives, but rather to arrive at the most well-informed conclusions. This might actually entail the "opposing" opinion being the correct assessment. It takes intellectual and emotional maturity to acknowledge that we were wrong. What part of you needs to be right? Which parts are you willing to let go along this journey? Which could evolve now that new information leads to an evolving personal context?

And which refuse to change? To those stubborn parts of you, give them a big hug. It may yet not be the time to peer into the shadow lurking beneath their obstinance. Development is an unwinding and unraveling process. It occurs in spurts, spirals, and steps and has an order of operations. Be gentle with your ego and continue to engage. It is a lifelong process.

Beyond Polarity: The Law of Three

The language of opposition and right/wrong are the zero-sum paradigm of win/lose thinking. It's the classic "us vs them" that allows us to associate our identity with a particular view and make opponents out of those who think differently. Sensemaking is an invitation to transcend this type of polarity thinking. Rather than over identifying with a particular position a good sensemaker enhances their ability to shift across the spectrum of ideas. This is the basis of dialogue, root words *dia+logos* meaning "to come together". In our modern times we are witnessing a period of extreme polarization because we have lost the ability to dialogue and instead allowed ourselves to become overidentified with particular viewpoints.

We get so locked in the current paradigm of left vs right, good vs evil, cool vs not, green vs dirty, that we fail to recognize that these are all just polarities. A polarity is a tension that can't be reconciled. Both the political left and right have distinctly different philosophical beliefs for how to construct society. The tension between the two views does not disappear. Regardless of where you are on the spectrum from far left to far right, the tension will always exist. This type of on/off, yes/no thinking is what dominates our world today. Our world is full of polarities like 1) justice and mercy, 2) activity and rest, 3) part and whole, 4) order and chaos, 5) progress and tradition, 6) love and hate, 7) climate doomer and climate skeptic, and many more.

You're either with us or against us. It's the red team versus the blue team. And all the other tensions that exist as battlelines drawn in the cultural sands. Our minds are primed for thinking about things as an "or" or a "versus". One of the primary skills to develop is being able to see beyond polarity and *unlock the thinking of both/and*. It's easy to get caught in the battle between entrenched sides. For a variety of reasons we're likely to pick this side or that. But for many of the issues facing us this polarity-based thinking is exactly what perpetuates the problem.

We must develop the skill of unlocking a higher order of thinking. As Ken Wilbur says, "we must transcend and include". As Gurjeiff says, "realize that phenomenon arises through three distinct lines of action: the holy affirming, the holy denying, and the holy reconciling". This is the thesis versus the antithesis, and the synthesis of both. Developing the skill of being able to tap into all three, rather than just the polarity, enables us to begin to think outside the box. It unlocks our ability to begin to see in new ways, imagine new futures, and to understand the relationship between two existing poles, holding the truth of *both* within us and even reconciling the tension between them. Unlocking the capacity to see the merits of all perspectives, even if we don't agree, is essential to effective sensemaking and allows us to understand multiple points of view and synthesize the best of each into a new one.

The Programming of your Mind

Human minds are incredible. From savants whose brains have hyper-optimized for a single endeavor to obedient mind-slaves who rarely have an original thought to the twisted thinking from the minds of history's most notorious villains, it is truly remarkable how flexible the human mind is. The *brain* is the physical organ that we can touch and physically changes over time through neuroplasticity. Our thinking and thoughts can be programmed; this is the essence of the brain we can't touch, our *mind* and its thinking, creativity, power, and ingenuity.

We're all programmed. As a part of the socialization process we receive a tremendous amount of information about what is and isn't appropriate. This is heavily influenced by our culture, class, and the political, moral, and spiritual beliefs of our parents and the wider community of humans in which we are raised. Inside the networks of our socialization there are rewards (or punishments) for thinking, feeling, and acting certain ways. Sociologists call this imprinting and we receive these influences throughout the various bonds and relationships of our life, though particularly during childhood.

So much of the information about what is and isn't desirable comes in the form of little packets of information called memes. While most think of memes as funny GIFs on the internet, the science of mimetics is the study of how information replicates and is passed on. It is modeled after genetics (it rhymes) where the passing on of human genes is determinant of our biological potential. Mimetics study how memes (information packets) replicate through the social environment and affect our thinking and doing.

In his book *Wanting*, Luke Burgis explains that much of what we do is mimetic. He explains that we are often copying behaviors in order to achieve a particular outcome. He differentiates between thick desire, action taken from our true deep desires (less common), and thin desire, which is replicating behavior in order to feel belonging and acceptance in some larger group identity. Thin desires often occur with consumption, like owning branded items, wearing the latest fashionable clothing, or buying the latest gadgets or smartphone. They are typically more ephemeral, passing in time like following diet fads, the latest fitness craze, celebrity trends, or participating in online challenges.

There is an endless number of people who seek to influence your identity, thinking, doing, and spending. People who seek to expand their ideologies, membership in their group, or market/mindshare. People waging war via identity politics. People who want you to buy, click, sign, donate, attend, post, and say what they want. This is the game of influence where playmakers try strategies to achieve their outcomes. It happens on the broadest scale through geopolitics and international relations and on the smallest scale with a social media like or micro-targeted ad. We must be ruthless and determined in self-examining how our own minds have been programmed by the many actors who seek to influence us. And never has it been easier for them to do so given the ubiquity of modern technology.

Information Literacy

As our lives continue to grow inundated with technology we open up more avenues to our influence through advertising, television, digital, and social media. Many people have become meme curators without realizing it, picking and choosing which memes they spread based on their assessment of how it will help them achieve their own agenda, which is often being liked, respected, or paid. Rather than thick desires and independent thinking, great masses of people are being programmed by actors spreading their agendas through ever more sophisticated tactics designed to hijack our dopamine and influence our behavior. By cultivating your skills at sensemaking and working to uncover how certain memes reinforce your identity, it will become more obvious where your mind has been programmed or weaponized. In doing so we free ourselves to develop our own informed assessments of what appears to be true.

Developing information literacy is essential in the modern world. First, you must develop awareness of the fact you're receiving information to begin with. This is building the self-awareness to notice *when* you are consuming information, which is challenging considering the volume of information we are exposed to. Then, it requires engaging with the information being presented in a way that maintains the independence of your meme assessment. By focusing on the agenda beneath the surface, you can begin to discern what this information might be trying to motivate, and determine where this information exists in relation to your reasoned beliefs. Rather than being ideologically captured, or simply resorting to meme replication because it's easier than being the kid who sticks out, info literacy is the willingness to stand for your own carefully considered critical thinking. That the mainstream media has an agenda should be no surprise and if you listen or read carefully you can quickly expose the loaded assumptions and phrases that tell you which issue framing they seek you to adopt.

Reprogramming your mind and keeping it flexible and open requires seeking out a variety of information across the spectrum. For instance, in writing this book I created a Twitter account just to follow all the leading climate scientists, changemakers, and thinkers who generally align with the ethos of this book. Yet I also know it's extremely dangerous for the mind to only see one type of information. Like wagons through mud, the more travel these neural pathways get, the deeper the ruts and more entrenched they become. Thus it was important I also followed the leading climate deniers and economic thinkers whose ideas conflict with the perspectives in this book. It is essential to consistently expose yourself to contradictory information sources and hold the conflicts with an unbiased mind to effectively determine which has merit.

Biases and Fallacies

If brains are likened to a computer, then sometimes code breaks or was written poorly but still made it past quality assurance into production. If we use a biological analogy, sometimes proteins are misfolded, nerves misfire, and a certain gene starts to express undesirable traits. Processes don't always work without a hitch.

In our physical brain we call these cognitive biases. In our non-physical thinking mind we call these logical fallacies. Together, the biases and fallacies represent common thinking errors that are robustly observed across people over time. They exist as an evolutionary process of our brains constantly looking for shortcuts. If we can arrive at reliable conclusions more quickly we expend less energy which is an evolutionary adaptation giving us more energy and advantage over others.

The biases (below) and fallacies (in the appendix) are both well-documented and difficult to avoid, though the process of learning about them and increasing self-awareness is the best method of revealing them in our own thinking as well as others.

Cognitive Bias	Description	How It Applies to Overshoot	How to Address the Bias
Confirmation Bias	The tendency to search for, interpret, favor, and recall information in a way that confirms one's preexisting beliefs or hypotheses.	Ignoring or dismissing evidence of ecological limits due to alignment with existing beliefs or economic interests.	Promote diverse sources of information and encourage open-minded engagement with evidence on ecological limits.
Dunning-Kruger Effect	The phenomenon where individuals with limited knowledge overestimate their own ability to understand complex issues.	Overestimating personal or societal capacity to deal with the consequences of ecological overshoot without significant changes.	Educate about the complexity of ecological systems and the serious impact of overshoot, highlighting successful mitigation efforts.
Optimism Bias	The belief that oneself is less likely to experience negative outcomes compared to others.	Assuming that serious consequences of ecological overshoot will affect other regions or future generations, but not oneself.	Emphasize personal and local impacts of ecological overshoot to foster a sense of responsibility and urgency.
Status Quo Bias	A preference for the current state of affairs and resistance to change.	Resistance to altering lifestyles or economic models that contribute to ecological overshoot.	Showcase sustainable lifestyles and economic models as feasible and desirable alternatives to current practices.
Ingroup Bias	The tendency to favor information and initiatives from one's own group or community.	Group identity influences perceptions of ecological issues, leading to polarized views and resistance to consensus.	Foster cross-group dialogues and collaborative projects to address ecological overshoot beyond political or social divides.
Availability Heuristic	Overestimating the likelihood of events based on their availability in memory, influenced by recent events or media.	Focusing on short-term environmental recoveries or events as evidence against the long-term trend of ecological overshoot.	Balance reporting of environmental issues to include both challenges and solutions, emphasizing long-term trends over isolated events.
Anchoring Bias	Relying too heavily on the first piece of information encountered when making decisions.	Initial information about ecological issues shaping long-term perceptions, making it difficult to update beliefs with new evidence.	Encourage continuous learning and updating of beliefs about ecological issues as new evidence becomes available.
Hyperbolic Discounting	Preferring smaller, immediate rewards over larger, future rewards, which affects long-term planning and decisions.	Valuing immediate economic benefits over long-term ecological sustainability, undermining efforts to address overshoot.	Highlight the long-term benefits of action today
Bandwagon Effect	The tendency to align beliefs and behaviors with those of a group, especially when many others are adopting the same beliefs.	Public opinion and behavior towards climate change can significantly influence an individual's actions and beliefs.	Showcase widespread support and action for climate change mitigation to encourage more individuals to join.
Negativity Bias	Giving more weight to negative information or experiences when making decisions or forming opinions.	Focus on negative aspects of climate change can lead to despair and inhibit action by fostering a sense of hopelessness.	Focus on positive actions and successes in addressing climate change to inspire hope and motivate engagement.

Practice: Bias and Fallacy Inventory

Take a few minutes to reflect on each of the biases and fallacies. Write down:

- if, and how much, you can see each active in yourself, or those around you?

- what are the places/sources where you see these most active?

- which one or two are worth giving attention to and how you plan to do that?

Make a commitment to devote several weeks to a single bias and make a game out of recognizing it in yourself and the world. When you notice it, practice a reframe of how you might correct it, and how that might change your thinking/conclusion, or not.

Developing the capability to recognize biases and fallacies in thinking, yours and others, is an essential skill in being able to transcend the common traps that our brain-minds appear to be wired for. This keeps us from seeking out information that confirms our thinking, preferring only near-term solutions, jumping on the bandwagon or to conclusions, and all of the other all-too-common outcomes of these mental shortcuts.

Systems Seeing

A global pandemic starts in one corner of the world and a few months later toilet paper can't be stocked quickly enough. A ship runs aground in the Suez canal backing up shipping and causing a shortage of containers around the world. A war on the Black Sea roils global energy markets making bread unaffordable for some Africans. A major cybersecurity attack on a cloud service provider wipes data across thousands of businesses, causing widespread disruption in digital services and financial losses. An unexpected frost in Brazil spikes global coffee prices causing café owners worldwide to raise their drink prices. Each of these real-life scenarios is best explained by examining the complex web of systems in which these events occurred.

In order to effectively comprehend these scenarios and the gordian knot of the polycrisis we must increase our systems literacy. Systems thinking is a holistic approach that focuses on our ability to perceive a system, its constituent parts, and how they interrelate with one another and interact over time. For the complexity of our many crises it is the tool that helps us to disentangle the many interwoven dependencies. It is a higher order of thinking that reveals the flaws in the traditional, linear approaches that make up the systems within which we often find ourselves operating. To train systems thinking we must develop our awareness of:

1. **Interconnectedness**: Recognizing that systems are made of interrelated components, where changes in one part of the system can have unexpected effects on other parts of the system.

2. **Holism**: Emphasizing the importance of considering the whole system rather than trying to fully understand a system through the parts its made up of.

3. **Feedback Loops**: Identifying and understanding positive (reinforcing) and negative (balancing) feedback loops within systems.

4. **Causality**: Looking beyond simple cause-and-effect relationships to more complex and multifaceted interactions within the system.

5. **Emergence**: Recognizing that systems can exhibit emergent properties which arise from the interactions and relationships among the system's components.

6. **Adaptability and Evolution**: Understanding that systems can evolve over time, adapting to changes in their environment.

Systems seeing is a lens that enables us to conceive the complexity of man-made and natural systems. It is an absolute requirement if we are to develop robust and nuanced understandings of what's true, why, and what to do about it. As we deepen our systems literacy we become more aware of potential systemic interventions and the trade-offs each of those solutions entail. While it will never give us mastery over the law of unintended consequences it encourages us to think about our efforts in larger contexts.

Mapping is an essential skill in systems literacy which involves us making mental maps of systems and how they work. Good maps, like causal loop diagrams and systems dynamics models, contain parts, flows, interactions, relationships, inputs, and outputs. Maps are useful tools in helping us conceptualize the complexity of a system.

> **Practice: Mapping** Pick a place you're at often, like a grocery store, restaurant, or gas station, and practice mapping out the *entire* system that brings the place/service into being. Another system you're highly familiar with is your home which is a perfect place to map the complex system that keeps it functioning.

Developing these tools is a lifelong process. These capabilities will grow you into a wiser human more adept at meeting the moment. Cultivating them will increase your sovereignty, individuality, and insight. There are plenty of books on each, some listed below, however the school of your life offers the best opportunity for you to develop these capabilities. As you sharpen the tools in your toolbox we can turn back to our main task in Part One of answering the question: what really is our moment?

Resources and Further Reading

- Sensemaking and Information Literacy: Wanting by Luke Burgis, Street Epistemology Online, The War on Sensemaking video series by Daniel Schmachtenberger, The Meaning Crisis Videos by John Vervaeke

- Self-Awareness and Ego: Existential Kink by Carolyn Elliott, Self-Observation by Red Hawk, Letting Go by David Hawkins, The Surrender Experiment by Michael Singer

- Systems Literacy: Cynefin by Dave Snowden, Polarity by Barry Johnson, Seeing the Forest for the Trees by Dennis Sherwood, Regenerative Development and Design by Pamela Mang, Ben Haggard, and The Regenesis Group

Last Chance

The truth is hard. It's difficult to look at and keep in sight. It is so much easier to look away. Why would anyone bring discomfort upon themselves? Why would anyone chance disrupting their convenient lives? Why ruin a good thing? Why threaten the construct that holds our ego and identity together?

It's not too late to turn around and put the book down. To back away from the ledge. Do you really want to know? Why? What's at stake if you read further and discover for the first time, or perhaps the tenth, just how bad it is and might get? What's at risk if you put the book down and continue on your way? What if the context in which you live your life and make decisions changes based on your assessment of the information that follows?

One thing I've considered perhaps more than anything else is: is ignorance bliss? Perhaps if you are invested in maintaining psychological or emotional comfort. Our greatest growth is found beyond comfort and the choice is yours in who you want to become. And yet when you're "on the other side of the door" it sure is nice to romanticize ignorance sometimes. It might be easier, but is it right? Do you want to sensemake more effectively? Do you desire to grow into your true potential? Do you want to Meet the Moment? If yes, read on and pop your bubble of ignorance, or what's left of it. Let's take a deeper look at climate change, overshoot, and the underpinnings of modern civilization.

As dark as it will get, anchor within yourself now that looking at the moment is worth it. That doing so is a commitment to what is good, true, and beautiful about this world. It's like cutting off a toxic partner, it will hurt in the near future, and bring greater joy later.

Five

Carbon Life Forms

"One does not become enlightened by imagining figures of light, but by making the darkness conscious."

Carl Jung

As you read this chapter, anchor in yourself the possibility that in order to become the most capable human adapting to the world as it changes, you must increase your ability to absorb difficult and challenging information. As you do so, allow yourself to be moved intellectually, emotionally, psychically, and spiritually.

It's important to first have some context on how our complex climate works. We also have to acknowledge that there are many things we don't understand. Just like space, gravity, the quantum realm, and the oceans, our global system of interconnected climate forces is animated by rules we only partially understand. Despite the limits in our scientific understanding, there is much we understand from robust, repeated observation that falls within the known laws of thermodynamics, chemistry, physics, meteorology, geology, and ecology.

It all centers around carbon. Literally. You and I are carbon-based life forms along with everyone else on the planet. Our planet is one giant carbon cycle passing on carbon in one form to the next over varying time scales. Between 286 million and 360 million years ago during the Carboniferous Period the planet was covered with algae, plants, dinosaurs, and all types of prehistoric creatures. As they died they fell into swamps and bogs and went through a 60 million year process of becoming coal, oil, and natural gas in the ground.

It was in the 19th century when we unlocked these fossil fuels by inventing technologies that allowed us to extract this extremely dense source of carbon energy to use as fuel. Whales around the world rejoiced as their oil quickly became obsolete. And fossil fuels turned out to be an extremely plentiful resource. The 20th century became an unparalleled period of human history marked by unprecedented economic growth in a debt-and-credit-based economy which encouraged consumption and the expansion of the global economy which now ensnares us.

It is an indisputable scientific fact that burning fossil fuels emits carbon dioxide and other greenhouse gasses (GHGs). As more GHGs are released into the atmosphere more of the sun's rays get trapped when they normally would escape back to space. As Earth's reflectivity decreases it absorbs more energy per square meter, trapping more heat in our atmosphere leading to what's called the Earth Energy Imbalance (EEI), the amount of extra sun energy that stays when it used to leave.

Our EEI is skyrocketing. For every 1°C of warming the air will hold 7% more moisture. That seven percent supercharges weather volatility creating more fuel for hurricanes, storms, floods, and yes, even snow. Increased atmospheric heat absorption raises ocean temperatures and leads to dying coral reefs and melting icebergs which will contribute to global sea rise. Meanwhile on land, hotter and drier land temperatures lead to increased forest fires as parched trees succumb to fire's deadly grasp and release their lifetime of stored carbon back into the atmosphere. This is but one of the positive climate feedback loops which may accelerate over time. And there's much, much more.

It's really quite easy to type all of that out.

Maybe you've read that bit before.

And it's pretty easy to read it as a list of facts.

But let's stop for a moment to really, deeply reflect on what this means.

It's more mothers screaming in blood curdling agony as their son is swept away in a flood. It's more children in the global south who will die ribs exposed, swarmed in flies, buzzards licking their lips as their food sources are priced out of a global market contending with food shortages where the rich will pay for the available food first. It's the trauma of having your whole town, your whole life disappear overnight and all of your earthly possessions and places of eating and being erased with no clear reason or means to rebuild. It's lamenting the choking smoke from fires a thousand miles away that taints the midday sun pink, sends asthmatics into fits, and sends us all fleeing the carcinogenic particulate-filled air. It's the 300 million people who live by the ocean, just as our hominid ancestors did to survive the ice ages, now driven to higher altitudes and latitudes as climate refugees follow in the footsteps of the many poor islanders whose homes were the first largely unnoticed-or-uncared-for casualties. Its rivers and beaches covered in dead fish and toxic algae blooms much farther than the eye can see. It's your feet walking crunch-by-crunch through a landscape that burned so hot it not only melted cars but the chance of life reemerging anytime soon. It's the twist of your stomach because you haven't eaten in days. It's your extreme grumpiness because the storms damaged the energy infrastructure so significantly that you haven't had power in three weeks. It's your shelves missing 50% of your regular purchases because of crop failures and disrupted logistics. It's temperatures that make travel virtually impossible.

It's coming for everyone. In his provocative book *Ministry for the Future*, Stanley Kim Robinson opens with a story about a wet bulb 48°C event in India which kills 100 million people. A wet bulb event occurs when the temperature in the shade of a thermometer covered by wet linen exceeds 35°C. This represents the temperature beyond which the body can cool itself, even while profusely sweating. Beyond wet bulb 35°C the human body begins to cook. Without air conditioning in places like India or Pakistan there is a serious chance of a mass mortality event. But that would never happen in the West! Until the electricity grid that we assume is a given buckles during a used-to-be-a-record-but-is-now-just-the-new-normal heatwave in Phoenix or New Orleans. Or further north in London or Chicago...

It's been said that climate change will be a video on a screen until one day you're filming it yourself. The effects of this are not theoretical. This is not conjecture. It is already happening. It's not just news on the screen. How many times have you watched someone say, "I never thought it could happen here." How many times? And yet if you're being honest with yourself, is that not how you're acting about climate change? Safely ensconced in our little bubbles until that bubble is swept up in a raging torrent of atmospheric moisture. Soon you, me, or a friend will play the fool uttering how we too didn't think it could happen here.

From ice cores and fossil records we have substantial historical evidence of how many parts per million of CO_2 existed at various points going back millions of years. The record shows clearly that there are substantial variations in GHG levels. Yes, CO_2 was higher in the past. What the record also shows is that these fluctuations took place over millions of years. The climate change that is driven by humans is playing out in the period since the Industrial Revolution. In just two hundred years we have so drastically altered the composition of our atmosphere that zoomed out across the last 400,000 years the CO_2 from modern industry is a straight vertical line off the top of the charts.

It's not that the climate is changing — always has been. It's *how fast* it's changing. Life and evolution are extremely adaptable. All plant and animal bodies could adapt to higher temperatures and an altered air composition over time. Time as in many thousands or millions of years. It takes many generations for nature to selectively upregulate sets of genes that express these new adaptations. The problem is that the pace of our fossil-fueled modern craze is moving far faster than our ability to adapt.

Energy Blind

Our standards of living are so incredibly high because in just a few short centuries we've drawn down millions of years of energy stored in the form of coal, oil, and gas. And as we do this, we've failed to connect modern economics to physical constraints. A critical mistake was made in the field of early orthodox economics, a mistake upon which our whole modern society is built: that labor and capital were the main source of value, diminishing the role of energy and physical resources. This has led us to rapidly increase labor, capital, and the efficiency of both over time while growing increasingly disconnected from the physical realities of this modern economy.

Everything in nature centers on energy. From mitochondria to photosynthesis to the functioning of our own bodies, energy is the currency of life that all biological systems are optimizing for. An energy surplus is an evolutionary advantage for growth, reproduction, competition, and all the basic functions of any species alive. Life operates through metabolism, the speed at which energy is acquired, transformed, and expended. An overactive metabolism, like our modern economy, will always in the long-term lead to a breakdown of healthy function.

Scholar Nate Hagens in his podcast *The Great Simplification* illustrates our energy blindness in great detail. He notes that economics has been blind to the fact of how much we've relied on fossil fuel energy to replace human and animal calories. By saving human and animal labor, we've relied on huge amounts of cheap fossil fuel labor equivalent to *500 billion human workers each year*. This has been drawing down the fossil fuel carbon battery at an unsustainable rate. Yet modern economics treats the availability of energy as just another good whose needs will be solved by the laws of supply and demand rather than facing the reality that the easy, cheap sources of oil have already disappeared leaving coal, gas, and dirty-to-manufacture-and-fossil-fuel-intensive renewable energy as the sources soon required to carry the load of our burgeoning global economy. It is likely that we won't run out of oil but we will continue to spend increasing amounts of energy to acquire the more difficult-to-acquire energy sources.

Prompt: Take a moment to look around your environment right now. Unless you're in the wild, you are undoubtedly surrounded by signs of the metabolism as it hungers. Consider all of the energy required to create and sustain the environment you're surrounded with right now.

Consider how every material in your environment was individually mined, transported, processed, and manufactured. Consider the energy for upkeep. Consider the energy required to keep your body on the move and in health. Consider the energy in your waste and purchases. All of this is the metabolic activity of the superorganism, of modern life hungering.

Traditional Economics Has Run Its Course

The field of ecological economics creates a clear picture of our current situation. The technological progress made in the last 120 years and all the efficiency that comes with it is due as much to energy and resource inputs as human ingenuity. Our energy sources have been so cheap and abundant for so many years now that we've forgotten that energy is what drives our society, not just brilliant technologists and industry titans.

This reality would actually be acceptable if our economic system tethered its money supply to energy and physical resources. Unfortunately, money is created out of thin air by banks. After we ended the gold standard and money was allowed to float, for every dollar, Euro, pound, yen, and ruble created it enters the economic system created as debt. Because we must pay back not just the principal but the added interest as profit to the loan holder, the nature of this economic system requires ever-expanding money, and thus ever-increasing energy requirements if the economic system is to continue as it is currently structured.

The Modern Lifestyle

The uncomfortable reality is the train of our Western lifestyle that we've grown accustomed to is on the tracks and it's not going to stop. We've forgotten how new our incredible abundance actually is. We're lulled into a sense that our material abundance is normal while failing to see the underlying reality: that everything in our modern lives is driven by fossil fuels.

Your food is sown and harvested by giant agricultural machinery which requires dirty, heavy industry to manufacture. It was transported by truck to a processing facility, then rail, then another truck, and finally into the hands of a stocker who drove their old carbon-emitting junker to work because they couldn't afford any better. The lights in the grocery store and in your house are likely powered by coal or natural gas. Your clothes, house, office, car, baby food, cell phone, books - your everything! would not exist without fossil fuels.

Climate activists are railing against governments for continuing to allow fossil fuel exploration. Many call for a total phasing out of fossil fuels. The uncomfortable reality is that there isn't a clear picture of how eliminating fossil fuels would work in a long-term sustainable manner for the current global population *at the level of lifestyle currently led in each country.*

Consider your life. How would it work without fossil fuels? Even in acquiring your basic necessities, if you follow the supply chains towards the raw materials, it's a staggering number of links in the chain that rely on fossil fuels to complete their part.

Green Growth

Even if you swap some of this story out for one with renewable energy it does not solve the problem. It is possible to consume significantly less, drive an electric car, have all electric utilities, never step on an airplane and still have a life that is heavily dependent on fossil fuels. There are many that herald wind and solar, electric vehicles, and the electrification of everything as the answer. But renewable energy, *while absolutely imperative to pursue,* is unlikely to replace our reliance on fossil fuel. FFs are cheap, still relatively abundant, and 90x more energy dense than a lithium ion battery.

Switching entire sections of the economy, or even just our entire global fleet of vehicles will require enormous resources that must be mined, transported, and manufactured using fossil fuels. When comparing the volumes of rare earth minerals required to manufacture even a single generation of wind and solar large enough to feed current energy demands with the known reserves, it quickly becomes apparent that it's highly unlikely we have the physical resources to sustain current energy consumption in a transition to "the green economy". And that's not factoring that renewables like wind and solar must be replaced, and thus remanufactured, a process that is currently fossil fuel intensive.

This uncomfortable truth is often ignored because it flies in the face of the trillions of dollars of investment that are pouring into the green economy. These investments are not misplaced. Without them there would be little reason to see how we might ween ourselves off the fossil fuel teat. And yet the sobering reality is that the rush to green solutions is in many ways just another example of the latest wave of capitalism at work, minting fortunes for climate do-gooders while refusing to accept a future that requires less energy. Sustaining our current economy with green energy is still fundamentally destructive for our biosphere.

Proponents seem to believe that green energy will replace fossil fuels, and they might entirely. If we do manage to swap FFs for greener sources of energy, without reducing our levels of material consumption, we will only succeed in powering the economic machine of ecological destruction that will continue to threaten our planetary boundaries. The evidence also shows that as we add more renewable energy to the mix it has not reduced FF energy consumption. Instead it has only added to *total* energy consumption. Our modern lifestyle is like going for a third, totally unnecessary plate at a holiday meal: we just can't but help ourselves to more.

The Ugly Truth

"The truth does not change according to our ability to stomach it."

Flannery O'Connor

Truth is a tricky thing. One person's truth can be another person's lie. Still, a life is well lived when we venture to understand what's true about ourselves and the world. The truth is often less convenient and rosy than we want to admit. The truth is hard. A life and a worldview absent the truth is a fantasy. Building our ability to stare down the truth and hold it in sight allows us to build the power necessary to meet what is *actually* going on.

The Ugly Truth is that oil is a wonder drug. We're addicted and blind to its many effects. Without oil the whole system will not power. No more plastic anything. No more road trips, airplane rides, or goods traveling long-distance. Imagine what that last point means to your grocery store shelf. *No more cheap anything.* Without oil the jig is up. And we can't let that happen. So we'll spend increasingly large amounts of resources acquiring FFs and electrifying everything else while month-by-month and year-by-year the engine keeps hurtling down the tracks, its smokestack bellowing out the GHG that scientific consensus says will undoubtedly raise global sea and surface temps.

There is *plenty* of oil still in the ground and when push comes to shove we will invent new ways to access previously-inaccessible reserves or entirely new methods to power the economic machine like hydrogen, fusion, or geothermal energy. The problem is that as we do this we turn the wheel of overshoot. Our endless pursuit of resources, consumption, and profit will lead to us experiencing tipping points for many of the planetary boundaries and the grim realities of existential risks-become-reality.

What about those scientists? They dutifully truffle off to the International Panel on Climate Change demanding change to politicians who are unwilling to say the truth: this can't go on. This. Our whole way of life. Our. Whole. Way. Of. Modern. Life. Cannot. Continue. As it is.

The facts have been clear for decades and none of these realities are new. In 1979 the Club of Rome released the seminal book *Limits to Growth* which laid out scenarios of how consumption and population would track with climate change deaths and pollution. Unbeknownst to the Limits to Growth authors, oil company scientists were coming up with similar projections in top-secret internal memos on CO_2 pollution tied to oil extraction and economic growth. Since then the observed data has trended shockingly close to their decades-old predictions. What was true then is still true now: that GHG emissions are only one large part of an even bigger reality of overshoot that toxifies our environment and threatens collapse.

The ugly truth is that we can even excuse fossil fuels from the conversation entirely — then look at the tremendous forces of resource extraction, manufacturing, transportation, land use, water use, chemical toxicity and ubiquity, and all the physical effects of our modern economy — and come to the conclusion that this cannot reasonably continue and still lead to planetary and human health. Something is going to break. The foundation is predicated upon the assumption of unlimited resources and our blind faith in our ability to innovate new technology to save us. When you consider the existential risks and the complexity of our many crises, we are loading a bullet into every chamber and playing roulette with the future of not just our species, but most species.

Stop and consider your reaction to this statement. What's present for you? Do you roll your eyes? Another "doomer". Another alarmist. It hasn't happened yet. Greta Thunberg said it would happen by 2019 and it didn't....it must not be real, right? Or at least the adults in the room will take care of it, right?

News flash: the adults in the room are not the ones in charge. The adolescents-in-charge have been captured by corporate interests because they were for sale to the highest bidder. Because we live in a culture that fails to connect us to that which is greater than us. Even in the far left wings of many Western country's politics there is significant hesitation to say the full-on heart-skipping gut-wrenching truth about our Moment because...the show must go on. And as the arc of this book progresses we'll examine just *what to do about this.*

Taboo and the Status Quo

Why don't the politicians, scientists, and media speak the raw truth? It has become a taboo to reveal how the modern economy feeds ecological overshoot in the mainstream media. Bits and pieces of the puzzle are present but never put together with the sobering clarity that draws the whole picture. Because the whole picture is a threat to the pervasive and all consuming nature of our global culture which pursues economic growth absolutely. At every level of the system, the superorganism of our society seeks to continue itself, blindly hungry to keep the machine providing extreme wealth to those at the top and allowing money to buy the luxury, comfort, status, and experiences that silence the ugly truth for ever greater numbers of humans.

Alternative narratives to the headlines of job-and-GDP-growth have become taboo because the contradicting reality is so foundationally inconvenient that most people lack the skills to be able to fully process this reality. Climate and overshoot denial are completely reasonable reactions to any information that seeks to threaten a system that on the surface is working quite well for billions of people in the developed world.

We'll pick around the edges of being able to move beyond denial in this book, and much more work on your end will be required. And that's a drag. I don't want to do this work. Probably neither do you. I have bills to pay and stress to relieve and my beautiful life to live. And why would I voluntarily be the first mover when everyone else is shoving more coal in the engine's burner? So the show goes on. Until it doesn't.

Impacts and Implications

There are a variety of forecasts that the global scientific community has rallied their attention around. Each of these models a scenario of different degrees of warming above the long-term global averages. It may not seem like a lot, a few degrees, but these are drastic changes to a climate that has been essentially stable *for all of human history.*

According to the book *Drawdown* by Paul Hawken, at 1.5°C of warming severe heat waves increase by 14%, sea-level rise will displace 69 million, an ice-free summer will occur every 100 years, biodiversity loss will affect 4-8% of various species, 80% of coral reefs will be lost, and 35 million people will be exposed to decreases in crop yield.

With just 0.5°C more of warming, severe heat waves will be 2.6x worse affecting 37% of the global population, 10 million more people will be displaced by sea-level rise, ice-free summers will be 10x more likely once every ten years, biodiversity loss will be 2-3x worse, 99% of coral reefs will be lost, and 10x as many people will be affected to reduced crop yield. At 3°C of warming by the end of the century, we could lose 50-70% of all species on the planet.

How does one read this as more than words on the paper? This is not abstract. It's not over there where the poor people are. It's here in the developed West in our waspy cocoons tucked amidst our rows of shopping centers and parking lots. The uncertainty of these scenarios is which path we are trending on and how fast we're moving toward that reality. It appears that 1.5°C of warming may have already occurred and 2°C of warming may be "locked in". It's not a question of if. It's a question of when. We have pumped enough GHG into the atmosphere that some scientists, certainly the most alarmist, are saying that a minimum +4°C is baked on by 2100. That means everything changes well before then. Even the most conservative climate scientists are growing more concerned.

As I sit here writing this in the woods of Northern Michigan, we have just witnessed the previous summer of unbelievable weather in 2023. Record heat waves were observed in Japan, China, Italy, North Africa, England, Canada (near the Arctic Circle), the United States, and perhaps most shockingly South America *in the middle of winter.* Record flooding has occurred in Libya, Italy, Sweden, Greece, Taiwan, and the list goes on and on. Fires have ravaged Greece and most shockingly Canada where 8% of the world's Boreal forests have burned in a few short months. And while the United States has fortunately avoided a direct hit, there has for the first time been a Category 5 hurricane in each global water basin supercharged by the same record water temperatures that have led to mass coral bleaching and mortality events. These water temperatures are so warm the charts have to be extended so the Y-axis could fit the data: "off the charts" is not a colloquialism, it's our reality. Crop failures have occurred in Ukraine (grain), India (rice), Georgia (peaches), and many others. Meanwhile, global ice extent is at its lowest or second lowest in most places, another case where the trend line is shockingly lower than the previous record. Finally toss in the news that it's not just single species that are going extinct, entire branches of the tree are disappearing.

You might be thinking "I bet this guy is a lot of fun at parties...". I get it. This is downright fucking depressing. It'd be so much easier to look away, to go back to Tik Tok, the latest sports or fashion season, or the newest episodes of insert-your-favorite-show-here. To numb or self-soothe is a very natural and understandable reaction to this information. It's so much easier to look away. Time to tuck this book away as another you made it partway through.

But that doesn't change the nature of the problem. Ignoring, soothing, or continuing in cognitive dissonance doesn't change your relationship to our Moment. Each of us must take responsibility for what's ours in this equation: to each our ability. It is essential that you stay with whatever discomfort you feel around the conversation. That discomfort is your ticket to "being the change" as Gandhi said. And yes, there is some cause for hope, and we'll explore that later. Back to the task at hand: wallowing in the sheer magnitude of just how bad it actually is.

Resources and Further Reading

- Drawdown by Paul Hawken

- Books by George Tsakiridis

- Unsettled: What Climate Science Tells Us, What It Doesn't, and Why It Matters by Steven E. Koonin

- Capitalism in the Anthropocene by Jason W. Moore

- Deep Adaptation: Navigating the Realities of Climate Chaos by Jem Bendell by Jem Bendell

- Hospicing Modernity by Vanessa Machado de Oliveira

- The Great Simplification by Nate Hagens

- At Work in the Ruins by Dougald Hine

- The Heat Will Kill You First by Jeff Goodell

Six

Sensemaking the Polycrisis

Counter Point

"But...is it really *that* bad? How can we be so sure? Does this "science" withstand scrutiny? And my cousin so-and-so knows all about this stuff and he told me that it's all a scam..."

There are many arguments you hear refuting climate change. They'll call the ideas in the last chapters "climate myths" or the #climatescam. It is essential to <u>not</u> dismiss these claims. We must examine all available information if we are to effectively engage our sensemaking. If we are to be rigorous in pursuing the truth then we must leave no stone unturned. Otherwise we are ideologues attached to a particular outcome, unwilling to seek and genuinely assess the validity of contrary evidence. Regardless of who you come to read this as — a climate denier, skeptic, aware, activist, or doomer or as a proponent and beneficiary of modern industrial capitalism, an overshoot fanatic, or economic charlatan — I encourage you to loosen your grasp on this identity and belief set. If you're a denier (and still reading) go back and reread the last capter. If you're an activist, can you really hear the following criticism?

We must operate in good faith while we attempt to consider all the sides. The outcome of this sensemaking is not inconsequential. We are addressing a topic which on one end trades in theories that lead to the end of our civilization and on the other end speaks of domination by globalists bent on reducing population under the guise of climate regulation. The stakes are high in either direction, conspiracies abound, and each of us must make sense of this in the limited time we'll allow this conversation to occupy our attention. The following are some of the most popular claims about the falsehoods of the climate crisis:

Claim 1: "The climate's changed before. It's a natural phenomenon. Current changes are within natural variability."

Examining the Claim: While the Earth's climate has changed throughout history due to natural factors (like volcanic eruptions and solar fluctuations), the rapid warming observed over the past century is primarily due to human activities, especially the burning of fossil fuels and deforestation, leading to unprecedented levels of greenhouse gasses in the atmosphere. When we look at charts that show higher temperatures or atmospheric carbon in the past, we often fail to recognize that humans did not exist then. What's important to center is that the pace of change today is far more rapid than any previous reported period.

Claim 2: "It's the sun."

Examining the Claim: In the last 35 years of global warming, the sun and climate have been going in opposite directions.

Claim 3: "It's not bad."

Examining the Claim: The negative impacts of global warming on agriculture, health & environment far outweigh any positives.

Claim 4: "There is no consensus"

Examining the Claim: You'll often hear that "97% of scientists agree" and while this highly-publicized figure appears to be overstated, and who can really survey every *qualified* scientist, there is broad overarching consensus the planet is warming and substantial agreement it's caused by humans.

Claim 5: "The climate has been cooling in recent years, not warming."

Examining the Claim: Short-term fluctuations in temperature do occur in one region or time frame, but the long-term trend shows that the Earth is warming. The last decade was the warmest on record, and each of the last four decades has been successively warmer than any decade that preceded it since 1850.

Claim 6: "1934 was a hot year in the United States. It was hotter this day in X year. It's been cold out recently."

Examining the Claim: Cherry picking data will always show it was substantially hotter or colder in one place than another. Weather and climate are distinct concepts. Weather refers to short-term atmospheric conditions in a specific place at a specific time, including events like rain, snow, cold snaps, and heatwaves. Climate describes the long-term average of weather patterns over a significant period, usually at least 30 years, for a particular region or the entire planet. A cold day, or even an unusually cold season in a specific location, as well as a much hotter day in the past, does not contradict the global trend of rising average temperatures.

Claim 7: "Animals can adapt. Plants breathe CO2."

Examining the Claim: Global warming will cause mass extinctions of species that cannot adapt on short time scales. While CO2 is a necessary nutrient for plants, excessive CO2 in the atmosphere leads to weather conditions that adversely affect plant growth. Recent studies do suggest plants and trees are adapting to higher C02 if extreme weather doesn't kill them first.

Claim 8: "But fires are good for forests."

Examining the Claim: While it's true that fire plays a natural role in the ecology of certain forest ecosystems, such as those adapted to periodic low-intensity fires, the context and intensity of these fires matter significantly. Climate change is leading to hotter, drier conditions in many regions which can increase the frequency, intensity, and scale of wildfires beyond historical norms.

Claim 9: "The human body can adapt, we can build up our tolerance to heat."

Examining the Claim: Human adaptability has limits, especially when considering the rapid pace and extreme nature of predicted temperature increases due to climate change. While it is true that humans can acclimatize to a range of temperatures, extreme heat poses serious health risks, including heat exhaustion, heatstroke, dehydration, and exacerbated chronic health conditions. Moreover, not all populations are equally equipped to adapt, with vulnerable groups (such as the poor, elderly, children, and those with preexisting health conditions) being particularly at risk.

Claim 10: Climate science, doomers, and woke liberals want to destroy our economy and way of life through regulation and green policies.

Examining the Claim: That any group wants to destroy our economy and cause substantial human suffering is hyperbole, at least not easily probable. However, attempts at regulating and changing the nature of our economy through green policies will require substantial behavioral change and sacrifice that many will oppose and call government overreach. This claim is more true than most.

These claims and others are prevalent amidst a vocal group of climate deniers and skeptics active in the media who present facts, figures, and charts in a convincing manner. In almost every case the "scientific" evidence of deniers can be effectively refuted. From the outside-in it looks like both climate changers and deniers are both claiming their science is correct. Upon closer examination it appears that the climate-denial-meme-creation-engine is disingenuous about how it uses the data to create doubt. It's unfortunate that most claims can appear credible on the surface until a chart is expanded to show the whole picture or the full context of the claim is brought into view. Still, it's important that we gird ourselves from subscribing to either ideology that would have it do our thinking for us. We must always be ready to hear contradictory evidence and reassess our position.

Regardless of what we see on Fox News or read on Zero Hedge, the evidence is overwhelming that anthropogenic (human-caused) climate change is both real and accelerating. The IPCC in 2021 said that it "is unequivocal that humans are the cause of climate change." Climate deniers will quickly point to a range of predictions that have not come true as evidence that it's all a giant conspiracy to control the populace and restrict freedoms. The reality is the climate system is too complex to forecast with perfect precision even with our advancing scientific technology. And while the conversation is often limited to carbon and GHG, when expanded to include the many aspect of overshoot, like water quality and soil health, the larger picture comes into view.

Even after we have looked at the top ten denier reasons and examined their validity, we should not assume that "science is settled". Yes, most scientists agree. And still there is plenty of room for error and evolution: such is science. The aim of our sensemaking is not to be right beyond certainty. Rather it is to act according to our most informed and reasonable assessments.

Game Theory

Just like risk analysts or statisticians we must take the whole climate picture into account and assess the most likely scenario. Game Theory is a branch of mathematics that explores strategic interactions among decision-makers and helps predict the behavior of different countries and entities as they negotiate and implement strategies to mitigate environmental impacts. It treats the polycrisis as a multiplayer game where each participant (country, corporation, person) has to decide whether to cooperate (by reducing emissions or production) or defect (by prioritizing economic growth over environmental considerations).

Game theory helps us analyze conundrums like the "free rider problem", "the tragedy of the commons", and "the prisoner's dilemma" which all wrestle with human decision making.

Thinking about the polycrisis as a game, we must look at all the facts from the proven science about the link between fossil fuels and GHG emissions to the observations that our economic pace is not slowing down and weather records are being broken in quick succession and consider the chance that we're not heading toward world-changing climate change or existential risk? Game it out. What outcome seems most likely to you? Double check your conclusion. If you assess a lower likelihood of significant ecological overshoot, is that because it's what you prefer? Or because that's the logical conclusion? It's important to come to the conclusion on your own. Not because you lean left or lean right or if it's acceptable (or not) in your social group.

When we expand our scope of consideration to include all x-risks, probabilistically, the logical conclusion is that the polycrisis is trending towards a higher-risk scenario, quickly, with serious implications for each of us.

Beyond Belief

Belief is a word that is thrown around often. What is the nature of belief? Let's examine something that's true: gravity on this planet. It's never faltered. It appears to be a law driven by the physics of mass. Is gravity something you *believe* in? If somebody said it like that, would you think it's kind of strange?

Is climate change something you *believe* in? Do you believe in climate change the same way you believe in a higher power or an afterlife? Both a higher power and heaven are concepts that cannot be physically seen and so require faith. We believe in Jesus, Allah, Buddha, Shiva, etc... and it requires some leap for us to go from scripture to believing in these divine beings.

The same cannot be said for climate change. It is not a matter of belief. Your belief doesn't make it any more or less real because it's already happening. It's observable and measurable. You can touch the scorched forest, notice that the weather in your place was different than it was in the past, or hold the grieving mother in a way that is far more physically real than believing in Zoraster (or your higher deity of choice). That doesn't mean that our divine beings can't be felt, experienced, and even perceived in the 3-D world. But theirs is the realm of belief. The climate crisis and ecological overshoot is our tangible reality.

I don't *believe* in climate change. I *assess* its likelihood and evaluate the latest trends. I observe the signs and signals in my own place and feel the weather patterns changing over time. That's not to say there isn't a place for "god" — we'll get there later. If we are to Meet the Moment we must take in the facts and scrutinize the latest reality of our situation. It is only from the clarity of what's actually occurring that we can evolve to take appropriate action. Overshoot must not be a matter of belief like the issues of abortion or gun control, which are debates centered on morality and ethics. We must ground ourselves in the evidence while keeping a scrutinizing eye towards the quality, funding, and agenda of said evidence.

But We'll Change

I hope so. Truly. This book is written because there is a viable path towards personal and societal evolution. But let's look all the way down the barrel. What evidence do you have that people will forgo their relaxing evening to educate themselves about the issues? What evidence do you have that people will, en masse, stop going on their vacations to fly less? What evidence do you have that all of the people will opt to do the hard work of growing food and raising chickens rather than run to the shelves? What evidence do you have that reductions in consumption will be widespread? Or that people are willing to be more uncomfortable on behalf of some future? Why would any of this happen when the very behaviors that are driving overshoot exist because that's how we cope with the disconnection caused by overshoot itself? Who has time for this?

In my observation of human behavior, these and many other behavior changes will not happen voluntarily. And by the time we're forced to make changes it'll be too late. If we don't change, our civilization might collapse just as every empire of antiquity from the Chinese dynasties to the Mongolian, Persian, Egyptian, and British empires all collapsed due a combination of economic, political, social, environmental, and climate factors. As in, all of the existential threats that loom today over not just the US or China but the whole global civilization.

Perhaps we're smarter now with all our information and technology. Perhaps not. We're betting a lot on our unproven abilities to manage natural and human systems of unprecedented scale. Either way, adaptation requires lead time. If our individual and collective responses lag the felt effects of overshoot there simply won't be enough time to build the resiliency required to absorb the shocks to come.

The bulk of the science is clear. I encourage you to do more digging. As you do so, keep your sensemaking hat on. Search for the truth regardless of your previous beliefs. What you will find from the leading researchers is shocking. It's hard to handle. The first step of the journey is looking at the hard truth. But before you go looting or on a hedonistic binge or take to asceticism in a mountain monastery somewhere, consider the following journal questions.

> **Prompt:** What's at risk if you really come to the conclusion that collapse is likely? What feelings arise when you consider collapse? Who are these feelings directed at?

Resources and Further Reading

- Inconvenient Facts: The Science That Al Gore Doesn't Want You to Know by Gregory Wrightston

- Apocalypse Never: Why Environmental Alarmism Hurts Us All by Michael Shellenberger

- The Moral Case for Fossil Fuels by Alex Epstein

Remember, it's important to expose yourself to all sorts of ideas, pro and con, in order to do your best sensemaking!

Seven

In Technology We Trust

Anybody can use tech, that is easy; but to use tech to the right degree, and at the right time, and for the right purpose, and in the right way – that is not within everybody's power and is not easy.

Adapted from Aristotle

W e got ourselves into this mess but it could not have happened without technology. With our opposable thumbs, creating tools is one of the most fundamental and distinguishing characteristics of the human species. The progress of human civilization can be told as much by the evolution of technology as by culture, war, or politics. The bumper sticker on our species' vehicle might read, "Why'd we do it? Because we can!"

Technology has always been a double-edged sword. There are few examples of humans refusing to adopt new technology. We're hungry for new benefits — convenience, efficiency, unlocking new capability — and seem to never allow our consideration of the trade-offs to significantly stem our adoption of the next generation of technology. The printing press, steam engine, A/C electricity, light bulb, telephone, refrigeration, pharmaceuticals, computer, internet, and now AI have each revolutionized our world, significantly reshaping the landscape of how humans live, work, and relate. This track record of success, one that is picking up exponential speed, has led to the total ubiquity of technology in our modern world. The inundation of technology in our lives is so complete that it is not surprising we commonly believe that technology will be able to continue solving all of our challenges.

The rallying cry is that tech that will suck up carbon from the atmosphere, clean up environmental degradation, unlock new or previously inaccessible resources, enable full electrification to replace all fossil fuel processes, and heal our bodies from the inevitable effects of all this industry.

But technology won't save us alone. Without significant behavior change the geo-physical limits of our planet will inevitably create greater constraint on the narrow-sight-ed-dollar-sign-in-eye-balls ambitions of the modern global economy. Yet there are many people who not only believe technology will save us, they are rushing as fast as possible towards it. Nowhere is more prone to magical thinking than our unbridled optimism for the role of technology as savior. This movement is often called Accelerationism or Techno-Optimism.

Techno-optimism is the belief that previously unimaginable technology can contin-ually improve and profoundly positively impact human life and the planet. This per-spective holds that the clear risks and negative impacts associated with technological development can be effectively managed. Techno-optimism is underpinned by an unwa-vering, sometimes blind confidence in human ingenuity and the power of innovation to overcome obstacles and create a better future yet is blind to to the many trade-offs and unintended consequences of so many exponential technologies emerging at once.

With the precariousness of the polycrisis and the world approaching multiple ecolog-ical tipping points, techno-optimists are willing to ramp production and dive humanity head-long into artificial intelligence and machine learning, biotechnology and genetic engineering, nanotechnology, quantum computing, space exploration and colonization, 3D printing, internet of things (IoT) and smart cities, and yes, even renewable energy technologies. They are betting the house on black. They are playing the highest-stakes poker with our biosphere on the line, wagering that these technologies will end the crises before the crises end us.

We must strike a very careful stance in our relationship with technology. We cannot go back to the pre-industrial age as many of the most ardent "doomers" prefer. A reversion to that time will come with significant suffering for the billions of people who have come to rely on technology. Yet at the same time we must *massively* reduce both our production and consumption of technology to reduce the geophysical pressure on earth along each step of the production cycle. Parts Two and Three lay out *who we have to become* in order to actually do this.

We must place our technology in service to life, rewriting the rules of engagement for what is and isn't appropriate and healthy use of technology. Tech is power. Power must be wielded responsibly. This theme is so popular in movies over the last decades because they strike a chord of truth and resonates with a fear and eventuality we all feel. Healthy rules of engagement must emerge naturally from a new collective ethos ushered in by cultural change rather than legislated by tops-down authorities.

Right now technology is not broadly in service to life. Much of the emerging and exponential technologies are chasing the good life. The executives will make billions, investors will get paid handsomely, new factories and servers will be built and maintained, and the economy will be stimulated as we enter our bright utopic tech-enabled sci-fi future. The largesse of these ideas is perhaps best displayed by our obsession with becoming a multi-planet species. Our determination to colonize Mars, a planet that is not remotely hospitable to life in the way Earth is, is a testament to the modern ethic of disposability. Finished with this planet? Move to the next one.

The most important point to orient to, and what often gets lost, is the emphasis on who is using the technology. It seems we have simply adopted the "build it and they will come" mentality without first considering who is showing up to use the tech. Tech is not in service to life because the users are not in service to life. As we come to rely more heavily on tech we will continue to lose the primacy of our relationship with the natural world and with it all of the developmental experiences that evolve us at the level of being. As always, it circles back to the inner game.

What is all but guaranteed is the continued devaluation of earth and its occupants as technology enables us to further disconnect human living from ecological health. This will continue to load the geophysical powder keg as we kick the can down the road rather than look in the mirror and do the hard work of changing our beliefs and behaviors. Rampant, unrestricted technology is a symptom of adolescence. The question an adult considers is not "can we?" but "should we?" whereas the untouchable and invincible adolescent careens forward without regard for the consequences of their actions.

Technological innovation is essential for any way forward. We must give great attention to developing and deploying new technologies in a manner that is just, humane, responsible, and always in service of life. And we must not place all our hope in tech and come to a new relationship with what is truly necessary, and not.

Prompt: Consider what is beneficial, harmful, and indulgent about your relationships with technology as it is interwoven into your life. How much are you hoping that technology magically saves the day?

Eight

Prophecy: Trouble on the Sea

H ow did we not see this coming? Many did. Our unique moment in time is not a surprise. The origins of the current polycrisis are decades and centuries in the making, the result of the long slow march of cultural evolution, technological progress, and economic development. This moment is a result of the economic and cultural myths we have chosen to bind ourselves to. All the forces of culture, politics, economics, and exponential tech seem to be accelerating on an inevitable collision course. The PSI in our pressure cooker is increasing.

To some this was not unexpected. Mystics and scholars alike have shared stories that point to 2020 to 2040 as a time unique in its potency, calamity, and thus potential for human evolution. A few of the many prophecies include:

- **"The Fourth Turning"** is a theory developed by William Strauss and Neil Howe, proposing that history unfolds in cycles of approximately 80-90 years, called "saecula," which are divided into four stages or "turnings": the High, the Awakening, the Unraveling, and the Crisis. Each turning reflects a distinct phase of societal mood and behavior, culminating in a crisis period that reshapes societal structures and values. According to this theory, we are currently in a Fourth Turning, a time of significant turmoil and transformation that could lead to a redefined societal order.

- **The Mayan Prophecy** of Katun 2 Ahau is part of a broader system of time-keeping that includes predictions and reflections for each cycle of the Mayan calendar. A Katun is a period of approximately 20 years, and "2 Ahau" refers to the ending day of this cycle which is associated with specific prophecies. The Katun 2 Ahau prophecy often speaks to themes of change, such as shifts in power, social transformation, or renewal, reflecting the cyclical understanding of time and history inherent to Mayan cosmology.

- **The Shambhala Warrior Prophecy,** rooted in Tibetan Buddhism, speaks of a time when the world faces great turmoil and degradation. In this current era, Shambhala warriors—enlightened beings embodying compassion and wisdom—emerge to guide humanity through its darkest hours. These warriors use non-violence and the power of insight to bring about change, healing, and unity. The prophecy is metaphorical, urging individuals to cultivate inner strength, awareness, and a heart-centered approach to life's challenges, emphasizing the potential for personal and collective transformation through spiritual practice and mindful action.

- **The Archaic Revival**, a concept popularized by Terence McKenna, advocates for a return to the holistic and sustainable ways of ancient and indigenous cultures to address modern society's crises of disconnection and environmental degradation. McKenna suggests that by embracing ancient wisdom, shamanic practices, and altered states of consciousness (often facilitated by psychedelics), humanity can reconnect with the natural world, foster global unity, and initiate a spiritual awakening. This revival is seen as a necessary step toward healing the rifts within ourselves and our societies, promoting a more balanced and interconnected existence.

- **The Prophecy of the Eagle and the Condor** is an indigenous prophecy that symbolizes the potential unity between the technological, mind-oriented ways of the Eagle (representing the North) and the intuitive, heart-centered ways of the Condor (representing the South). It foretells a time when these two paths can merge, leading to a new era of balance, healing, and mutual respect. This prophecy calls for the integration of different worldviews and the harmonious coexistence of diverse cultures, emphasizing the importance of bridging gaps between technology and spirituality, and between different human societies, to achieve a more holistic and sustainable future for the planet.

In their own interpretation, all signaled this particular 20-year-ish period where the stakes are high. These are trends that have been at work long before our parents were a twinkle in our grandparent's eye. Forces that shaman and religious ascetics could discern using their superior clarity. Cycles that have repeated themselves through history and trends that historians and scholars can delineate through time. Taken together we are guided by these sources to consider just how important this period is and what will happen when we lean into the possibility of working together to Meet the Moment as a people and culture.

Yet we don't need Miss Cleo to tell us that these are precarious times. All you have to do is read the news for a week and you will undoubtedly see the threads of every part of the polycrisis in news of the economic, social, health, educational, energy, and environmental crises, geopolitical tensions, supply chain and production challenges, political instability, and our deep cultural and ideological divides.

Some moments in history are more important than others. Ours is one. At the dawn of exponential tech, at this critical intersection of modern economics and ecology, there is an open window for us to act. It is a critical juncture beyond which we will lock in certain realities that cannot be put back in Pandora's Box.

Nine

Visible Signs? Or Confirmation Bias?

After the loss of a long-term life partner I spent the summer of 2022 road tripping around the West coast. In case you're wondering, yes it was in a big, old gas guzzling Lexus SUV and yes I find that problematic (but great for car camping). One leg of my wander brought me out to California and to the majesty of the Giant Redwoods, a place that has existed in the desires of my imagination for many years.

As I got slightly lost on the way up to the forest I stopped at a gas station to confirm the GPS' nonsensical directions. When the gas station attendant gave me directions he ended by saying "good luck". I didn't think that much of it at the time. But immediately after the road began to ascend in altitude I understood what he meant. The tall pine trees quickly turned to blackened toothpicks. The ground lush with wildflowers and vegetation became a putrid tan color devoid of anything except the ashy remains of what once was.

Mile after mile I climbed, air sucked out of my lungs, grief-stricken with tears rolling down my face as I drove through the remnants of the Kings Canyon National Park wildfires. Vista after vista opened up to reveal the totally crispified landscape. I stopped to get out and fly my drone only to discover the sheer immensity of the fire beyond the next ridge in sight. What was supposed to be a dream come true was tainted with the loss of this stunning forest. The Sequoias themselves are fine, they were saved through herculean efforts. Hooray? There's an eerie feeling being in a forest so thoroughly scorched that you feel life will not return the same there for many, many years.

This was neither the first nor the last evident sign of a changing climate on this trip. Earlier in the trip I had driven through dry riverbeds, empty arroyos, lakes where water lines fell much further below the distance the docks had already been extended down to. Outside of Santa Fe visiting my friend in Pecos I met the remnants of the largest fire burning in the world at that time, the Hermit's Peak Fire, which was accidentally set when a controlled burn spiraled out of control in ultra-dry conditions. It was here on the land of a community I visit often that I stared up at the sky in midday and found myself able to stare straight into the sun, its typically eye-damaging rays blocked by the smoke that turned the sky into an eerie orange sherbet at high noon. Every few days I crossed into a new landscape ravaged by forest fires, each time feeling another gut punch at the loss of another delicate ecosystem.

More recent travels have continued these trends. It seems I've been chased by heat domes, dodging tornadoes and hurricanes and leaving regions only to have them swallowed by floods shortly afterwards. It is this continuous experience, seeing the very tangible outcomes of ecological overshoot, and feeling the visceral pain of the leading indicators that will all-too-soon become more commonplace that has led to writing this book as perhaps the smallest action I can take in contributing to our evolutionary adaptation.

And while my travels are part of the problem, despite my attempts at offsetting the impacts, it has also exposed me to the astonishing beauty of the this planet, and of humanity, in ways that have only deepened my connection to all that is worth saving and to my convictions about our need to do the internal work, covered next in Part Two.

If you're paying attention, the signs of what's coming are everywhere. I can no longer look away. Can you?

Part Two: Reconnecting

"The hardest thing is to live richly in the present without letting it be tainted out of fear for the future or regret for the past."

Sylvia Plath

The natural world is beautiful. Life is a stunning miracle we cannot explain. It is stupendous in its magnificence, admirable in its resilience, and enchanting in its possibility. For all of its many drawbacks, our man-made world is also gorgeous. Our varied architecture, cultures, and people are all incredible in the fullness of humans expressing creativity, imagination, and Spirit. Despite everything we've covered in Part One, the world is utterly valuable.

The beauty of the world, of your world, in the everyday livingness of human being and relating deserves nothing less than our total presence and full rapturous love. Humanity is fully redeemable, and worthy of it. Humanity, not the economy, but humans, are worth saving. Though we all are accessory to overshoot, the vast majority of humans are good-hearted, existing with similar desires for belonging, safety, purpose, and connection.

The natural world is worth saving. It deserves our care and protection. It is the magnitude of our ability to see all this beauty in the world and to love one another that makes the stakes of our moment so high. There is so much worth it to lose.

Ten

Gone For Good

M uch has already been lost. Web search "lost species" and you'll find plenty of articles chronicling the latest species to be added to the extinction list. So much so that scientists have ample evidence we have entered the Sixth Mass Extinction. While the first five extinctions were caused by natural crises like volcanic activity, asteroid impacts, and ice ages, this Sixth event is entirely caused by humans. At a pace not witnessed in any fossil record we are losing species far more quickly than the background rate. With 40% of land converted to food production and only 3% of land left untouched, humans in our pursuit of profit and convenience are causing a biodiversity crisis that is erasing whole branches of the evolutionary tree and permanently altering the geology and hydrology of our ecosystems.

The diversity of life that makes our world stunning, beautiful, endlessly fascinating, and most importantly, ecologically functional, is disappearing before our teary eyes. What used to take eons is happening in decades. Right now as you read these words habitat is being cleared to grow feed for greenhouse-emitting cows - but multinational fast food restaurants need quarter-over-quarter growth, right? It will never be more than facts and figures to the person who has not truly awakened to the living breathing creeping crawling undulating budding swaying chirping roaring purring flapping trickling essence of the more-than-human beings we share this tiny rock with.

As long as "I" am the center of it all we will not humble ourselves enough to have our being cracked open in a way that we become the chirp of the morning birds, the miraculous birth of a new baby blue whale, the agony of another chainsaw blade ripping through our woody flesh, and the last desperate gasps of a fish poisoned or cooked alive in record-setting ocean temperatures. As long as we live in a dominator culture that prioritizes economic development and GDP growth over ecological health, we will continue our fundamental disconnection from life.

The concept of a zoo epitomizes the way modern society sees nature: locked up and available for exploitation at our whim. We designate small portions of land that are off limits for development and welcome to vacation. The very act of visiting nature to get something, a breath of fresh air or a shot for our social feed, is the extractive mindset itself. Nature does not exist for us. It simply exists for itself. But nature will not always be the same. Much like our world will never go back to pre-COVID there are thresholds we are crossing from which there is no return. These thresholds will usher in the vaporization of whole ecosystems. One way to really grasp this reality is to make an Overshoot Bucket List looking forward across the thresholds of what's at risk and feeling the call to connection before it disappears.

Practice: Make Your Overshoot Bucket List

1. Start by considering some of the natural wonders that you would like to see in the world.

2. Now imagine how these places might be affected by climate change and ecological overshoot. Do a bit of research. Are you surprised by just how much is at risk?

3. The ones that are at high-risk of being impacted will go on your Overshoot Bucket List.

What's on the endangered species list? What fragile ecosystems like the jungle or the reefs are sensitive to a rapidly warming climate? What cities on the ocean are vulnerable to rising ocean levels? What islands are disappearing? What places like the scorched forest or the desertified land will be so irreparably changed that they are essentially lost forever?

The purpose of this exercise is to connect you more deeply with all that's at risk. Not what we've lost but what we will lose in the future. As in, you might never get the chance to build a physical connection with these creatures or places because they won't exist *within your lifetime*. The further our disconnected society continues without awakening to the rights of non-human species and the inherent value of the commons, the more likely it is that many of your overshoot bucket list items will soon be added to the list of what's gone.

Grief

Loss is a part of life. We cannot lose what we are not connected to. Right now someone on the other side of the world just lost their parent or child but since we are not connected with them we do not feel the loss personally. Loss is personal. We lose loved ones. They pass on. They move. Relationships fall apart. We lose jobs, houses, and precious items.

Part of what fuels our current predicament is that we are no longer collectively connected to that which sustains our life: the living photosynthesizing respiring swimming flying world we are a vital part of. The less our society is connected to the living world, the less we have to lose.

It wasn't always like this. Go far enough back up any family line and you will find ancestors whose intimate, sensual connection with the living world was a core part of their existence.

This way of being inherently gestured towards revering the circle of life and having a literacy of the land. Back when nature's stock market was the ecosystem and its server farms were fields teeming with wildflowers. As Western Civilization and colonial empires spread across the world over the course of many centuries there has been a systemic erasure of cultures that worshiped their sustainer of life. Goddess-worshiping cultures were eliminated under the guise of witchcraft or strategically absorbed into the major religions. The major religions also sanitized themselves of their own feral, wild roots as they groomed themselves to fit a world driven by economics and science.

Slowly scientific thinking replaced magical thinking, mystical experiences, numinous nature, and enchanted encounters with the wild. The world morphed from one that knew the importance of an animate world existence to one that was mechanized with parts that could be understood through reason alone. As science and economics broke everything down into a process or part we sucked the life out of it and lost connection with the living forces that speak to our souls and inform us of our place among the complex system of life.

Since the start of the first industrial revolution we have grown more disconnected from nature. As more and more of our ancestors were compelled by economics to seek the benefits of progress, they left the countryside and fields for offices and factories. We gradually became accustomed to bricks, concrete, buildings, and streets instead of fields, streams, forests, and meadows. Nature was quickly relegated to manicured parks with square edges and the destination of weekends off or vacation, hardly the immersive experience required to open one's heart to the true miracle of the sentient world around us. We surrendered our agrarian past to industrial agriculture and lost a connection to the land that our ancestors could not have survived without. The longer this has taken place the farther removed we have become from the physical realities that support and nourish our society. As we dive deeper into what it means to Meet the Moment, we'll grow our ability to subtly acknowledge this reality and realign how we live our modern lives in ways that reconnect us to the heart of what's been lost.

Absent a connection to nature, it's easy not to grieve for the loss of our precious natural world. Something happens in a heart that's deeply connected to their land. It has the capacity to grieve when other lands are destroyed. This is the basis of empathy. When I drove through the scorched forest of the west I grieved not because it was my place but because I could see and feel this loss through my heart that is intimately connected to the treasured forest in my place, the one that I've shed many tears to over its decimation by logging. But to a human who doesn't experience true, deep connection with their place it's next to impossible to fully feel the depth of loss and grief associated with the many places and species across the world that have been irreparably damaged or permanently lost as an outcome of the cold, blind, and hungry economic machine.

Despite the utter gut-wrenching mind-bending life-shattering depths that grief can bring, it is one of the most important emotions we can experience. It signifies just how deeply we love and how connected we are to that which is worth shedding tears over. To be without grief is to not have loved and lost. Ecogrief, as it's called, is the natural outcome of connection to all that's being lost amidst our ecocidal society.

But to grieve first requires that we open our hearts for nature connection. As modern Western humans we are largely deprived of the opportunities for this connection to blossom because we lack sustained and frequent experience of nature. Our lives are hermetically sealed. We rush from our sterile homes to our sterile cars to our sterile offices; wash and repeat. Only 20% of the U.S. population lives outside an urban area. 2007 was estimated as the first year half the human species lived in urban areas which is expected to rise to 66% by 2050. When food comes from the store and nature is kept, mowed, sewn, trimmed, removed, and grown we have reduced our natural world down to its constituent parts. It becomes somewhere to escape to for a vacation or day hike, an overshoot bucket list adventure, but always a temporary retreat that ends with the return to stop lights, blue-lit screens, and drywall. As products of our environment it's no wonder we feel such a disconnection with our ecology. If a world does exist where human society lives in greater harmony and balance with nature, it will not occur without a proper reconnection to life. By reestablishing connection we not only grieve for what we've lost, we grieve for all that is no longer possible in the future.

One day a headline species like the rhinos or polar bears will disappear. And I'll grieve what we had and lost. And I'll also grieve for what will never be again. Like children born today who will never snorkel the colorful fireworks of a tropical reef teeming with life or enjoy the pleasure of walking through an old growth forest. All that has been or will be lost is worthy of not just our attention - but our lamenting.

> **Practice: Lamenting** is an indigenous practice that involves going into nature alone to speak of the pain, loss, and injustice one sees in the world. It is a practice of being in relationship to that which we lament and expressing our wish to restore balance and harmony to it.
>
> Your task is to go out into nature and lament. When it seems like you've lamented enough, go further. Going beyond what might seem reasonable is part of the practice.

By lamenting loss we allow the key of who we grieve for to unlock our disconnected hearts, stirring within us our human capacities to feel a deeper connection with all that's at stake. My own journey with eco-grief started years ago when the magnitude of our ecological crisis came into view. As the effects of modernity on particular species and ecosystems became apparent I felt my field of connection and care expand. As it did, grief activated my lamenting and jump started the work of reconnection highlighted here in Part Two.

Resources and Further Reading

- The Smell of Rain on Dust: Grief and Praise by Martin Prechtel

- Active Hope: How to Face the Mess We're in Without Going Crazy by Joanna Macy and Chris Johnstone

- The Wild Edge of Sorrow: Rituals of Renewal and the Sacred Work of Grief by Francis Weller

- The Work that Reconnects by Joanna Macy

Eleven

Towards a Spiritual, Deep Ecology

The Earth is alive. Of course the trees and animals are alive, we can see this. But the Whole Earth, the entire planet, is one sentient being with some type of fully-incomprehensible yet undeniable intelligence. It is more than just a celestial body holding all the other little bodies. The Earth dreams, talks, and moves just as we do. Some say we are a fractal of the Earth itself.

We understand the life cycle of a star, but what of a planet? Why has life emerged so fantastically here yet we have no other obvious examples of it in the enormous universe we've developed the capability to peer into? And the deeper we explore our world the more miraculous science tells us it is. Trees network with each other and share resources through mushroom's underground mycelial networks. Scientific research in the field of morphogenic resonance suggests that when a flower is cut on one side of a field it "warns" flowers on the other side of the field. Symbiotic relationships exist between bees and flowers, host fish and cleaner fish, birds and larger mammals, and countless other relationships we haven't yet discovered. Despite the 21 species that just went extinct in 2023, we discovered nearly 1,000 new subspecies. The vast variation of life on this planet, despite all of our effects on it, is a testament to the stupendous intelligence of evolution. How does this happen?

Developed by scientists James Lovelock and Lynn Marguils in the 1970s, the Gaia hypothesis suggests that organisms coevolve with their environment. As the theory goes, all life forms are part of one single living planetary being called Gaia. In Greek Gaia is the primordial deity and ancestral mother of all life. She gave birth to the sky (Uranus), the mountains (Ourea), and the sea (Pontus); everything is said to stem from her fertility. Similar personifications of the Earth Mother are present in many traditions to honor this fundamental understanding. In this view, all of the living beings on the planet, including plants and animalia, are like fungal fruiting bodies from the mycelial web of Gaia's womb.

Ancient cultures around the world, before the advent of our major world religions, practiced forms of spirituality that believed the divine permeates all of nature. Because their world was far less technologically advanced than ours, they were less distracted by advertisements, push notifications, crosswalks, and glowing blue screens. They lived closer to the land in a slower pace of life that afforded, and required, greater contact with the natural world around them.

Through this intimacy, cultures all over the world developed a deep reverence for the natural world and sets of practices that are surprisingly similar. How is it that each of these cultures began to realize the importance of the annual turning of the wheel, the passage of our Earth around the sun, the seasons, and the rhythm of the Moon? How is it that most of these cultures developed an intimacy with their landscape that supported the concept of balancing human needs and ecological health?

What they knew that we have now forgotten is that the Earth is eminently alive and full of Spirit. The living world is full of God. Religious scholars would call this animism, the belief that everything is alive. And for those who lived off the land they could actually see, feel, and hear that this is true. And so can you. This is a capability that helps you *feel* the Earth and its creatures, develop a connection with them that graces the divine within you and others, and is capable of giving you glimpses of the numinous life force behind the veil. It is not just inherent within the sensory features that come installed in your model of Homo Sapien, it is your birthright and an important step on the developmental journey to becoming an adult and fully functional human being. It's as if for thousands of years we knew this intuitively and developed cultures and spiritual traditions that encouraged this *way of being* and then when the industrial revolution started we threw out our operation manual in favor of a different set of ideals.

Something happens when you share unpressured time in deep nature. Not just a couple hours in a park, which *is* great and important, but after a few uninterrupted days at the minimum your nervous system resets. It adjusts to the rhythm of the land, to the cyclical chirping of the morning wren, the temperature at it fluxes throughout the day, the uneven ground welcoming your ankles and leg musculature to remember their true function beyond flat soles and floors. Your senses sharpen. You begin to move with more attention and the little details of the soil and tree bark begin to look more interesting and relevant. The body awakens and slows down. And nature begins to talk. It begins to sing its song of wind brushing through branches, the sullen bellow of a fallen log, the suspicious caw of crow above head, and the flirtatious trickle of the stream. You begin to hear. Not just the physical sounds in your ear. But the dream of the earth. Your dreams come alive and full color. Time begins to warp. It moves slowly, or not at all - but passes more quickly too. You begin to get lost. There's a memory in you that murmurs back to an intimacy with nature your DNA still recollects and yearns for.

Well, maybe. That's the possibility. And it's available even if you don't cloister yourself in nature for extended periods of time. But today we live in such manicured and regimented lives that getting out into deep nature is repulsive to many, inconvenient to say the least. There will be bugs and dirt. There's no shower so you'll begin to smell your own scent. The ground where you sleep may be uneven. Something will be uncomfortable. If this description is uncomfortable to you, if you feel some aversion to it, it's a welcome invitation to the growth possibility within you, and likely for all of us (certainly me) to some degree.

Do not feel ashamed. We are all products of our dominant culture that today fails to foster deep intimacy with nature by default. Why? Because nature is free. It doesn't drive the perpetual growth machine, unless it's being exploited. Time spent in nature, save for the gear you'll buy, reuse, and get tremendous value out of, is antithetical to our growth-oriented culture. Because the more time one spends *in nature*, the more it creates perspective about the world *out there* - civilized, convenient, productive, and bustling.

Nature is inviting you to go into the wild for three uninterrupted days. Oh that's quaint. I read a book and it told me to take three days off work to go into the wild. But when was the last time you did? What's your excuse for not doing so? If three days is easy, how about four or five days? Somewhere inside you is a point of resistance about going to spend phone-unplugged fully-connected time in nature. Is it a lot to ask? How come?

Resistance is your life journey's road sign to come closer to what's uncomfortable.

Then the voices pop up in your head. "Will I get bored? I'll surely get uncomfortable. Seems like a waste of time. I wont' get anywhere. I won't be getting ahead. I'll get dirty. It's dangerous." And on and on. These thoughts are the symptom of our disconnection.

They are the result of our reliance on modernity's comforts where money can be traded for full convenience. But anytime there's a trade, there's a trade off. It's not just money we're trading when we buy our comfortable life. The silent cost is our connection to the natural world that sustains our life. And so the thought of uninterrupted time in nature can approach abhorrent to some. You mean I can't post it on Instagram?!

It's not easy to simply go out in nature and get reconnected. One could wander out into the woods for three days, spend the entire time thinking about life, sports, or politics and drift back out of the woods having entirely missed the opportunity for connection. Because deep nature is difficult for us to experience on a frequent basis, an essential practice to begin is to develop a sit spot. This is a location close to where you live that you visit on a daily basis for a few minutes. It could be your stoop or a spot in a park. Wherever it is, it is a place that you visit with the intention of learning and connecting. As you deepen into the available connection with place over time, you begin to see how it changes through the seasons and start recognizing not just a robin but THAT Robin. This is possible even in a metropolis. Simply sitting under one tree is... yea, I know. You don't have time for that. Shame...

Practice: Establish a sit spot

1. **Choose Your Location**: Find a peaceful spot in nature that resonates with you, ideally one that is comfortable and you can visit regularly.

2. **Visit Regularly**: Commit to visiting your sit spot at regular intervals, whether daily or weekly. Regular visits help you connect more deeply with the natural rhythms and changes of that particular environment.

3. **Observe and Reflect**: Each time you visit, spend time quietly observing the life and elements around you. Take note of the wildlife, plant growth, sounds, and seasonal changes. Reflect on your observations and how they affect your body, thoughts ,and feelings

Where My Feet Are

"Humankind has not woven the web of life. We are but one thread within it.
Whatever we do to the web, we do to ourselves. All things are bound together.
All things connect."

Chief Seattle

Nature connection practices help us find humility in the web of life rather than an egoic determination to dominate it. You can find many practices listed in Appendix One. How do we return to nature? We must look to the indigenous as carriers of this way of being we have actively suppressed. The history of how indigenous cultures were and are currently being treated is repulsive. But not surprising. Over the last thousand years there has been a systematic attempt to erase those that are living in accordance with nature's laws. Because those who do won't exploit nature to drive progress or profits. Their beliefs threaten established religions and expanding markets. The level to which the eradication has occurred through the vociferous and violent elimination of pagan and earth-connected nature-intimate cultures is a testament to how serious of a threat they actually are to colonialism, liberalism, religion, and capitalism.

At the core of this way of being is *relationship*. The indigenous have a saying, *Mitakuye Oyasiin*, which means "all my relations". Said as a prayer and a greeting showing respect, it is an invocation that speaks to the deep feeling of connection one can have to the web of life that connects us to everything around us. It's our connection to the ancestors whose shoulders we stand on. To our vast web of family, friends, community, and our family of human brothers and sisters. To the animate world of four-leggeds, two-leggeds, winged ones, finned ones, , and all the rocks, trees, and grasses. This understanding is innate and intuitive because it is felt. This birthright is fostered. It is given respect, nurtured, and makes a centerpiece of an entire way of life.

And it's dangerous. One whose very own blood bleeds the sap of trees does not exploit the forest. One whose very own tears are no different from the river or ocean habitats does not pollute the water or pump it to dry oblivion. One who hears the whisper of the meadow grasses does not pave it over into concrete. One who is connected to the soil where the food and resources come from takes only enough, never "just a little bit more". This way of relationality is the medicine for our disconnection. It is the invitation into human existence that sacralizes the material world. It is an awakening to Great Spirit, to Mystery, to God, the Holy Spirit, the Godhead, the All, the Tao, the Divine, the Holy Spirit, the Unnameable Ineffable Intelligence that offers to each of us in every moment the opportunity to expand the scope of our humanity through greater relationship. As we do so our hearts expand as does our compassion, care, and conscientiousness. This is the promise at the core of every major religion.

The downstream effects of this type of awakening to ecology, "eco-awakening" as it's called, is not productive for the dominant modern economy because the resulting expansion of personal context often leads one away from mindless consumption, rat race competition, and *ego*centric living. Whether it's a purposeful repression or the byproduct of the system and its momentum, our society reduces the opportunities that facilitate true, deep ecological awakening.

Critics are correct in pointing out that it's not all beauty in the indigenous record. Brutality, savagery, and treachery were also commonplace towards one another. That this occurred is a testament to some of our inherent human tendencies that when left unchecked can get the best of us. Mature, adult societies do not wage war on others, nature, or themselves. They exist in dynamic equilibrium with their places and people. I'm unclear whether we've ever had a true example of this, and yet know and feel this possibility exists within our species as the outcome of our higher, more evolved nature. We are the ones who decide, either consciously or unconsciously, what standard we choose to live and become.

Reclaiming Indigeneity

I write carefully here with the sensitivity of a white man who has no intention of culturally appropriating what is not mine. I've spoken to indigenous elders from multiple cultures about the topic of reclaiming indigeneity. Nothing will erase the centuries of appalling blood-stained history and the treatment of our Native and traditional peoples.

A short personal story. My people have been in the United States for a long time. The latest my people arrived was 1850. The earliest my people arrived was two ships after the Mayflower. Always in the North, you can track their slow migration West as territory was colonized. My 13th great grandfather was the founder of Hartford, Connecticut. My other grandfather was the first Governor of a colony. They were the colonizers no doubt.

Eventually they wormed their way through Ohio, Iowa, and many settled in Michigan, where I consider home.

Like many, I'm a white European mutt. I'm English, Irish, Welsh, Scottish, German, and French Canadian. The British Isles make up about 80% of my blood. Before my ancestors became American colonizers, they too were colonized. It was just a long time ago. It's hard to say when. It could have been around 1600 when the Enclosure Act made public lands private or around CE 50 when the Romans came. Somewhere back in my British bloodlines were people who were intimately connected to the land. They lived, tended, respected, sang, survived, and struggled with the land.

We all have Indigenous roots in us. Because somewhere some time ago our ancestors were of the land. Until that kind of belonging was labeled savagery by religious and political ideologies those vested interest was disconnecting them to gain power, control, or profit, in turn atrophying our inherent human capabilities and usurping our natural rights.

The best way to honor the indigenous is to return to a way of being where connection to life is a central tenet.

It is time. **We must reclaim indigeneity.** Not to take anything away from the First Nations People. Or to claim native blood and the compensatory privileges we now afford the historically disadvantaged. It is they who have kept the fire lit while witnessing and suffering the consequence of modernity. The best way to honor the indigenous and their pain is to return to a way of being where connection to life is the central tenet of living. One could be an Indigenous Christian, an Indigenous Muslim, or Indigenous Atheist. An Indigenous Republican or Indigenous Democrat. Indigenous signifies that you have reconnected with the land. That you are of the land. That you once again feel the pulse of Gaia.

When traveling, I pick up trash as a tourist. Not because I want to look good or be an emissary for America abroad. It's with a sense that this little piece of land, here on a random corner in London or a dirt road in South America, is land that is alive and I'm connected to. This is always on offer. What might be the outcome of feeling a true, deep land connection? How might we treat it differently? What are the implications for the places we inhabit most of our lives? What are the downstream consequences?

It is also true that these ancestors lived shorter lives in tougher conditions with less convenience, health, and abundance. A common retort to praising "the old ways" is "would you really want to live back then?" The answer for most of us is of course "no". Reclaiming indigeneity does not mean a rejection of all technology like the Amish (though we'll see if they get the last laugh). It means looking out at the landscape and realizing that man and our society is only one feature, not the dominant feature, of our delicate home. It is venturing to balance our modern world while centering the best of who our indigenous ancestors were in their attunement to the land that sustained them.

Resources and Further Reading

- Coming Back to Life by Joanna Macy

- Of Water and the Spirit: Ritual, Magic, and Initiation in the Life of an African Shaman by Malidoma Patrice Somé

- Braiding Sweetgrass: Indigenous Wisdom, Scientific Knowledge and the Teachings of Plants by Robin Wall Kimmerer

- The Healing Wisdom of Africa: Finding Life Purpose Through Nature, Ritual, and Community by Malidoma Patrice Somé

Twelve

Religious Wisdom

If we are to once again belong to the land in a nurturing and mutually beneficial relationship then we must transcend the profane and once again sanctify our natural world. An examination of the major religion's texts reveals that philosophers and theologians across human history have all echoed the call for responsible stewardship of our home.

Christianity

"Every creature is a word of God and a book about God."

Hildegard von Bingen

Christianity recognizes stewardship of creation as a moral and spiritual responsibility treating nature as a gift from God which humans must protect and sustain. Genesis 2:15 says that humans are to "till and keep" the garden of the world, a verse that expands the sanctity of life, a core principle in Christianity, to our ecosystems and biodiversity. The Bible is filled with verses that discuss man's dominion (stewardship) over the earth, the ultimate ownership of the land by God not humans, warnings against misuse and neglect, and the interconnectedness of all creation. In his encyclical *Laudato Si': On Care for Our Common Home*, Pope Francis introduced the concept of integral ecology which links the care for the poor with the care of the earth and urges a comprehensive response to environmental degradation and climate change through a transformation of global ethical and economic systems.

Judaism

"In order for humanity to turn back from defacing the Earth, we must turn to behold the Earth's face."

Rabbi David Seidenberg

Through the holy scriptures of the Torah, Talmus, and later rabbinical writings, Judaism is deeply rooted in environmentalism, sustainability, and stewardship of the Earth. Tikkun Olam, which means "repairing the world", is a core concept that involves actions to improve the world *for all of its inhabitants*. Bal Taschit, meaning "do not destroy", prohibits the wasteful destruction of resources and has been interpreted to encourage conservation and sustainable use of resources. Shomrei Adamah, meaning "guardians of the earth", charges humans with the responsibility to protect and preserve the earth for future generations. Additionally Jewish law (Halacha) includes many laws about agriculture, animal treatment, waste management, and resource consumption which encourage a lifestyle that emphasizes the role of community and education in fostering respect for natural cycles and limiting environmental impact.

Islam

"In traditional societies, nature was seen as one's wife, but the modern West turned it into a prostitute."

Sayeed Nasr

The Islamic doctrine on environmentalism is rooted in principles found in the Quran, Hadith (sayings of Prophet Muhammad), and Islamic law (Sharia) which emphasize human's stewardship (Khalifah) over earth. Khalifah teaches that humans are entrusted by God to use its resources wisely and preserve them for future generations. The principle of Mizan, meaning "balance", teaches that God created everything in balance and that humans should not disturb the balance of creation. The principle of Israf, meaning "conservation and avoidance of waste", condemns wastefulness and encourages moderation in consumption. Other Islamic teachings highlight the sanctity of life, the importance of compassion towards animals and plants, and encourage collective efforts in tackling society's issues. The Islamic Declaration on Global Climate Change has called for all Muslims to reduce fossil fuel use and transition to clean energy, a decree that reflects how Islam is engaging with the environmental crisis.

Buddhism

"In all atoms of all lands, Buddha enters, each and every one, producing miracle displays for sentient beings."

Flower Garland Sutra

Though Buddhism does not have any official doctrine that directly addresses environmentalism, its core teachings of compassion, non-harm, and interdependence naturally extend to the living world around us. Buddhism emphasizes the interconnectedness and interdependence of all living and nonliving things and as such encourages a healthy reciprocal relationship with nature. Embedded here is the understanding that any harm done to others is ultimately harm done to ourselves through interconnectedness. This also aligns with the law of Karma which links actions to their consequences. Buddhism also focuses on karuna (compassion) and ahisma (non-harm) which together advocate for a nurturing attitude toward the welfare of every living being. Mati, or mindfulness, calls Buddhists to be aware and attentive to the present moment and thus to the effects one's actions are having on the environment around them. Sila (ethical conduct) comprises three aspects of the Eightfold Noble Path: Right Action, Right Effort, and Right Livelihood which call followers to live in harmony with the world. Among the many writings where these teachings are evident is the Lotus Sutra which teaches that the Buddha nature is inherent within all beings, mandating ultimate respect for all life.

Hinduism

"Economy without ecology means managing the human nature relation-ship without knowing the delicate balance between humankind and the natural world."

Satish Kumar

Hinduism's deep teachings on dharma (duty, righteousness) and the interconnect-edness of all life provide a domain for followers to live into many of the central beliefs. Ahisma, meaning "non-violence", is a core tenet of Hinduism that instructs us to be non-violent towards all living beings, not just humans. In Hindu scriptures Prakriti (na-ture) is highly revered and often personified as divine with many elements of nature, like Earth, rivers, mountains, and forests, being considered sacred and thus worthy of being kept pure. Hinduism views time as cyclical, rather than linear, which fosters a respect for natural processes and the importance of humans interacting with and not disrupting these forces. The practice of Yagna, or "sacrifice", encourages giving back to nature and the Gods and represents the reciprocal relationship between humans and nature. The Rig Veda, one of the oldest of the Hindu texts, contains many hymns to nature which emphasize the interconnectedness of all beings. The Isha Upanishad teaches the principle of non-possessiveness and respect for the world's resources. The Mahabharata discusses the importance of trees and forests and condemns their destruction. There are many other instances where the call to connection with place are present in the Hindu tradition.

Atheism, Agnosticism, and Secularism

"The Earth is a very small stage in a vast cosmic arena... Our planet is a lonely speck in the great enveloping cosmic dark. In our obscurity, in all this vastness, there is no hint that help will come from elsewhere to save us from ourselves."

Carl Sagan

Even for those who do not profess or doubt in a higher power, there are numerous strong arguments in favor of nature connection and environmental stewardship. Not believing in a higher power is not the same as being devoid of ethics and so atheists can argue that humans, with our incredible capacity to do harm, have an ethical responsibility to protect and preserve the environment for future generations. Atheists can argue that systems science has proven the interconnectedness of life systems and so protection of the environment is important for human well-being and survival. In the same vein of rational self-interest, it's abundantly clear that environmental degradation poses risks to human health, safety, prosperity, and happiness. The logic of a biosphere with greater biodiversity and ecological health is important in furthering the advances of science, science which continually demonstrates the negative effects humans are having on life. Finally with no belief in a higher power or afterlife, Atheists can view conservation as part of the legacy they leave for future generations and a way to give meaning to our existence.

***

Across the vast majority of spiritual and religious traditions we see the same theme of creation as a sacred act of God or as God/Spirit itself. In this understanding, the way we treat matter is the way we treat God. The word matter comes from the word mother revealing the link between our physical world and the life giver/sustainer. Together all the traditions suggest that respect for life, nature, and creation is a fundamental requirement of living a good life in relation to self, other, and higher power.

We must rediscover the ecological roots of the major world religions.

The growth of science as an arbiter of cultural truth has ensured that more people see the earth and all of creation as a set of parts that can be broken down into smaller parts and understood as such. Secularism's rise within modern democracies further cemented nature's place in our semantic schema as a public good, a tangible item to be managed and profited from. All of this has desacralized our living world. Ours is not a culture of life. Instead, in the void of our intimate, somatic, and spiritual connection with the flora and fauna we have a culture of death and destruction. Convenience and modern consumer abundance encourage us to ignore the ecological teachings every tradition has passed on as ecumenical doctrine and practical wisdom. There are many paths to the same practice of being in a deep relationship with Place.

Many have lamented that our world is turning more secular. I used to disagree, finding within myself the strong desire to see a separation of church and state. And while separation of church and state is a founding principle of most democracies, based on the natural law of self-determination, the more secular our institutions the farther we will get from resacralizing the world.

What we need is to rediscover the ecological roots of our major world religions. We must usher in an awakening of the Green Man, a universal archetype representing the cycle of growth, death, and rebirth, closely associated with nature, fertility, and spring which appears in various guises across many cultures and religions. We need to broaden the horizons of God's kingdom to once again include the more-than-human world.

The major religions account for 86% of the world's population. The role of organized religion in ushering in the change we need at this critical moment cannot be understated. Fortunately every tradition has long-established doctrine on the appropriate relationship to cultivate with nature. That a majority of the world has been lulled by corporations, adolescent culture, and consumption is not so much a failing on the part of religion as a testament to the enticing and corruptive power of greed, convenience, and luxury.

A return to deep ecology for each religion is a redemptive path to actualizing the ideal virtues each holds so dear in name. For what is required of us cannot occur without us being the best of ourselves. Regardless of what belief system, or combination of them, is yours, what's important is arriving here, where your feet stand, in recognition that yours is a sacred place full of life, beauty, and connection.

Thirteen

Story and Myth

The great religions are conveyed in parables and dialogues because the human brain is wired for story. When we hear a story it activates parts of our brain as if we are actually experiencing the story in real life. This is why we feel happiness during a comedy and scared from a horror movie. Stories are among the most powerful of our technologies. The more we tell them the greater their power.

We tell all types of stories. The narratives we tell about ourselves often explain who, how, and why we are the way we are. Many of these stories become self-fulfilling prophecies and the more deeply we believe the story about our creativity, or any other specific character trait, and repeat the story with conviction, the more likely we are to build a reality that reinforces that story. It will seem as if the story is true, yet ironically, is likely so because we told it that way. The same is true for the stories and myths that we tell about our world, how it works, and why it works that way. Many of these stories are indoctrinated through the school system and the process of socializing a particular national and cultural identity. They get coded as "that's just the way that it is" and reinforce themselves.

What we often forget is that stories are just a matter of perspective. They are memes passed down, fallible to memory mistakes and malicious manipulation. We were not present at the creation of many of the stories we explicitly and implicitly believe. Just as the bible was rewritten extensively throughout history, we too have the opportunity to rewrite the stories that have reinforced the status quo. Our opportunity is to tell entirely new stories that uproot the adolescent maladaptations of modern society and paint visions of what could flower from the flourishing heart of eco-awakened possibility.

That story binds us now is not a new phenomenon. It has always been myth that has congealed groups of people into shared understandings of nature, existence, knowledge, and the cosmos. Mythologists like Joseph Campbell and Carl Jung have, through great effort, detailed the many myths whose significance point to ephemeral truths about the human condition and our collective consciousness. These are the archetypes, cross-cultural themes, and enduring motifs that reappear across all known human time. Before our current social configuration it was the storytellers and mythkeepers, often the elders, who replicated the myth-as-meme from one generation to the next, ensuring that the vital cultural lessons of the past were handed down. In creation myths, wise parables, and fairy tales we encoded the wisdom that was too important to lose. Stories were the essential maps to humaning well. And in traditions the world over we came to understand the importance of the hero's journey, the mystical realities of nature, origins of existence, and many more of the important constructs that helped us find belonging through shared cultural context.

If modernity has done anything effectively it has severed the connection we had to the stories of our people. While technology allows us to record and replay stories, they do not teem with the same aliveness a direct transmission does. The oral lines teeming with life were broken by coal soot, Sears catalogs, and microwaves. Where once we were somatically alive and ecologically connected enough to receive the wisdom of the ancient cultural stories, now, if we are even lucky enough to be connected to sources of the ancient myths that teem with respect for life, we lack the full capacity to be able to understand their true meaning, to receive their teaching in our own body, and to extend our taproot into the unbroken lineage of those who lived with the land. There are a multitude of ways this disconnection has occurred, many mentioned in this book, with the end result that we forget the stories of modern economic monoculture are recent creations. We've even grown blind to the fact we're living out the stories ourselves, oblivious to the myths that lie at the very foundation of this current society.

There are many modern myths that actively shape the psyche of Western and world culture. The following seven myths help power the economic paradigm of overshoot:

1. **The Myth of Progress**: The belief that society is on a linear trajectory of improvement, where each generation lives in a more advanced, civilized, and prosperous society than the one before. This myth underpins many aspects of modernization and development but can overlook cycles of regression and the complex impacts of technological and social change. This is closely related to the Frontier Myth, and Manifest Destiny, which both celebrate expansion into and conquest of the frontier as a process of bringing civilization to wild lands.

2. **The Myth of the Hero**: This myth revolves around the idea that history and progress are driven by extraordinary individuals who rise above the ordinary to lead, innovate, or save their societies. It celebrates exceptionalism and individual achievement but can overshadow collective efforts, the contributions of ordinary people, and the roles of inheritance, societal structures, and the manipulation of those structures. This is closely related to the Myths of Rugged Individualism and the Self-Made Billionaire, which celebrates those who "pick themselves up by their bootstraps" through hard work and determination without much help. Somewhere in this constellation is the Myth of Meritocracy, the idea that social and economic rewards should be earned through talent, effort, and achievement, rather than through inheritance, social status, or systemic inequalities. All of this feeds the Myth of the American Dream, which suggests that anyone, regardless of their background, can achieve success and upward mobility through hard work and determination.

3. **The Myth of the Golden Age**: The belief in a past era of peace, prosperity, and harmony, often used to critique the present and inspire a return to the values and conditions of that imagined past. This myth is used to rally people against modern problems by idealizing a time that supposedly had none.

4. **The Myth of Capital**: It posits that wealth accumulation and capital are the primary measures of success and progress in society, suggesting that economic growth and consumerism inherently leads to social well-being and individual fulfillment. This myth is often blind to the disparities associated with unrestricted capitalism.

5. **Nature as an Infinite Resource**: The belief that the Earth's resources are inexhaustible and can be exploited without limits. This myth is driven by two centuries of industrial and economic development but is increasingly challenged by the geophysical realities of the polycrisis.

6. **Technological Utopianism**: The belief that technological progress will inevitably lead to a utopian society. This myth assumes that technological innovation is the key to solving social, economic, and environmental problems, leading to a better future for all.

7. **The Social Darwinist Myth**: The misapplication of Darwinian ideas to social and economic policy, suggesting that competition and survival of the fittest justify social inequality, imperialism, and racial discrimination.

This list shows the extent to which we have bought into a series of stories and repeated them *as if* they are true. And so they fulfill themselves and become our collective reality.

That these stories are readily observable in modern society is a testament to the power of story, but not to the perfection of the stories themselves.

New stories are needed, ones that vivify life, that tell of our species' great arrival home, now armed with incredible technology in service of life. Stories that animate the natural world, that build mountains out of mole hills, and mythologize the roly poly, the robin, and the raccoon. Stories that are themselves living invitations into deeper life connections. Stories that recenter nature and bring modernity into appropriate context. Stories that open us to grief and loss, hope and change, and connect us to the wisdom of meeting our deepest needs through prosocial behaviors.

Personal Myth

Each of us too has a personal myth. This is not something we dream up sourced from the whims of our ego. Just as places have a particular nature, our personal mythos emerges from our unique essence, what many call our Soul, in its own particular form. Our personal mythos chooses us as much as we choose it. In it is the invitation of living ever more deeply into our true gifts which reveal themselves as we go on our personal journey of healing, wholing, and Soul Initiation which we cover in the next two chapters. While our personal mythos is often influenced by the many universal patterns present in the archetypes of the collective unconscious, it is intertwined with our personal life path to create a totally unique expression. This is us as fractal, one totally unique part of the whole creational fabric. The possibility of our personal mythos is discovered through dreams, ritual, and nature connection as a mirror for our own true nature.

Language and Metaphor

"All language is metaphor."

Richard Rohr

Of all our innovations language is arguably the most powerful. It's hard to overstate how much language underpins our ability to effectively navigate the world. If you take a minute to think about it you'll realize that this book is all language, all of your thoughts occur in language, and everything around you has a word in your semantic map of the world.

Language is inherently metaphorical. The word "tree" is not the tree itself, but represents a shape, being, and structure that we experience as this thing called tree. Whether there is a tree in front of us or not, the word "tree" helps us recall the concept of tree. Every word represents that which it is actually describing.

The world is awash with metaphors. In his book *Metaphors* linguist George Lakoff expertly dissects many of the metaphors buried in the English language. In the opening pages he chronicles how the metaphor that *"time is money"* gets programmed into our language in a variety of sayings like "you *wasted* my time", "the flat tire *cost* me an hour", "I've *invested* a lot of time in her", "Is that *worth* your while", "you need to *budget* your time", and many more. Another relevant metaphor is *"the mind as machine"* through sayings like "boy, the *wheels are turning* today", "I'm *a little rusty* today", "we're still trying to *grind out* the solution", and "we're *running out of steam"*.

All of these phrases may be familiar and you understand their meaning. Yet hidden within our language are encoded messages, metaphors that subtly shape the nature of our thinking. The *time is money* and *mind as machine* metaphors both encode mechanistic and materialistic conceptions of both time and our mind rather than employing metaphors that reify life into our language. We desperately need to closely examine our language for the subtle beliefs loaded within. Changing our language transforms the very nature of how we relate to the world. Harnessing the power of language will enable us to recode many of the hidden assumptions of modernity.

> **Practice:** Practice **Conscious Langauging,** the skill of increasing your self-awareness around the language you use. Rather than blindly accepting the words and phrases you know, inspect them for the true etymological meaning or hidden metaphorical assumptions. As you do this you'll begin to choose your words even more carefully, thus constructing reality in new ways.

This changing of language can be difficult. Even switching from "spending time with you" to "enjoying time with you" is difficult for me. Simple shifts like moving from saying "problem" to "challenge" or "choose" instead of "should" can have big impacts on the way we communicate. And while it may seem like semantics, words matter. They create our reality!

Giving attention to the language we use is essential in shaking loose the programming that we have inherited. As language is the medium of understanding, this again highlights the importance of mimetics. How we receive, comprehend, and replicate packets of information has massive effects on our thinking, feeling, and doing. Cultivating the self-awareness and sensemaking required to Meet the Moment empowers us to rewrite our personal and collective narratives in ways that serve life. As we awaken ourselves to the tough realities of our world and our place in it, we grow our competence in telling new stories that inspire each of us to sense how we might reimagine the world as it is today.

Rewilding the Non Physical

Rewilding as a concept often refers to the efforts at reversing biodiversity loss, restoring habitat, and protecting species. While we need a massive effort to rewild our land, it is also our minds that must be rewilded. We must free our minds from the rows of desks in school, the white lines on the highway, the cubicle with your name tag, the square-gridded city blocks, sitting in a chair all day, and the multitude of other ways that modernity has shaped our living. We must resow our minds with language evocative of our ecological place in the world. We must imagine new metaphors that take back functions from the mechanized metaphor and reinvigorate natural understandings of the processes that govern life and the metabolism of our hungry economy.

To this end I have, wherever appropriate, infused this book with language and metaphors that seek to reassert the primacy of natural metaphors rather than mechanical. To rewild our language we must use more of it that reflects our deep respect for nature, expresses relationships in ecological terms, and challenges anthropocentrism by co-centering non-human experiences.

Resources and Further Reading

- Metaphors by George Lakoff

- The works of Joseph Campbell and Martin Shaw

Fourteen

Trauma, Healing, and Wholing

Much is made of healing and trauma in the contemporary personal development and self-help industries, and with good reason. Trauma may singularly be both the Achilles heel and greatest opportunity for humans on an individual and collective level. So what is trauma? Trauma is not what happens. Trauma is how we respond to it.

Two people were sitting in a commercial airline when it crashed. Both miraculously survive. One feels victimized by such an awful tragedy, internalizes the nightmarish scenes of flames and bodies, and lives as if everything changed for the worse after it. The other sees it as a miracle, feels the grace of God, and moves forward with a new lease on life. One is traumatized, the other is not. Trauma is not what happens, it's how we internalize our response to those events.

Trauma is the thought patterns and psychological mechanisms we develop after an event to keep us safe. It is the parts of ourselves that we learn to repress. Or the parts of ourselves that go into overdrive to protect us from threats. Trauma is real. It is a rational response to challenging, stressful, injurious events whether the events are physical, emotional, or psychological. It is often noted that mammals seem to have built-in mechanisms for shaking off trauma, literally. After a near-death experience, mammals in the wild often shake, which is commonly accepted as a mechanism designed to ensure the stress, cortisol, and fear do not get programmed into the body and nervous system.

The link between trauma and the body is overwhelming. Awakening the bodies, particularly the physical body, is an absolutely essential developmental step. We must be able to discern the "felt sense" or our bodies. If we are to heal then we must work towards being able to feel our emotions fully. The deeper our connection with sensuousness and somatic experience the greater our capability to perceive and work with our trauma.

There are many different types of trauma and these exist at a variety of different layers. Trauma can be *acute*, from a single event, or *chronic*, from prolonged exposure. It can be *complex*, when multiple traumas stack, or *secondary*, picked up from other's trauma. It can be *developmental*, from our formative years, or *historical*, experienced by specific cultural, racial, or ethnic groups. *Generational* trauma is passed down from generation to generation. The science of epigenetics shows how trauma from our grandparents passes down to us directly through our genetics, beyond the more obvious familial programming transmitted directly from our parents.

And because organizations and cultures are made up of humans, these larger containers also contain trauma. Traumas live in the collective memory of our species and many identities are coded with painful memories of the past. These traumas live in our stories, monuments, language and phrases, actions, and in the collective conscious. These realms are where our collective dreaming emerges from and are the source of many of our unembodied and subconsciously present traumas.

Taken together, these personal and collective traumas are ever present until we embark on the delicate and essential process of unwinding and integrating these traumas. We will not begin that work now, though you can never truly Meet the Moment without having completed some requisite amount of trauma work.

And yes, YOU have trauma to heal. We all do. It is the very nature of being human to pick up trauma along our life's journey. Even the most idyllic childhoods with the most attentive parents and the most perfect social environment with every need taken care of will still develop trauma. Buried in each of our wounds is a gift that when fully integrated into wholeness leads us to deeper understanding, wisdom, and resilience.

The real luxury is having the time, attention, and capability to address your trauma. It is a privilege to be able to do so as it requires at the bare minimum some psychological safety, and is greatly supported by having the lowest two rungs of Maslow's hierarchy of needs fulfilled. It is significantly more difficult to be able to process trauma when your attention is focused on acquiring the basic necessities. Confusingly, and like many things in life, it is entirely possible to swing too far to the negative pole of healing trauma. You can become addicted to healing your traumas, a personal-growth junkie who spends all of their time and attention peeling back the endless onion of Self. The reality is that the work is never done. There is always more to heal.

Healing for healing's sake is useful to some extent, but is it practical in the larger context of our Moment? There is a threshold to reach, the Minimum Viable Healing, which is the minimum amount of healing required at any one time to render one's Self effective at moving forward with the practical, tangible realities of life. The more our choices become ecocentric, emerging from our Soul, the more the course of our healing and wholing moves parallel to that which orients back to service to others. Yes we must first put on our own oxygen mask, yet also be wary of getting distracted or addicted to the high of that pure oxygen.

Heal and Whole what's in the way.
Allow your life to guide what's necessary.

Our task is not to remove our traumas, or forget them, but "to whole" them. Whereas healing is designed to make trauma go away, the purpose of wholing is to embrace our past experience, integrating the various experiences of our life. Healing focuses on symptoms while wholing seeks the hidden reservoir of energy in the mind, body, and spirit, and through self-awareness enables our transmutation into the healthier, more whole version of ourselves.

There is much to heal and whole within, even just related to the many micro-aggressions we experience as a result of modernity. To Meet the Moment, we must move beyond our own victimhood, blame, or anger to reach a balanced place within ourselves that sees the many actions of people in our world as a natural result of modern society. By seeing the world through a developmental lens, we begin to understand that because each of us is on our life journey navigating the rigors of modernity to the best of our ability. Instead of falling into judgement of ourselves and others, we begin to accept the complexity of our moment and why people may behave in certain ways. In being "trauma-informed", we can respond in ways that are more compassionate, neutral, and healthy.

The most important thing to remember is that healing and wholing are not the end in and of itself. It is always *for* something. It has a utility beyond the obvious personal benefits of being a person who is operating from less trauma and psychological needs. The purpose of this work must be for us to come back out into the world a healthier and more whole version of ourselves capable of meeting the moment. The healthier we are the less likely we are operating from old scripts and programming that would have us act and operate in certain ways that perpetuate the status quo. From our wholeness we will continually embody new ways of being that unlock the previously-unseen potential of life surrounding us.

The Wellness Trap

Healing for healing's sake is tempting and somewhat beneficial. It's easy to get caught up in the wellness industry when everyone's brother and best friend is a life coach. The steady rise of the wellness industry, including all of the spiritual modalities, should come as no surprise to an observer of the sickness in our culture. Like most things human, the proliferation of coaches, programs, diets, modalities, practices, gurus, books, pills, and you name it is simply a response to our environment becoming more toxic over time. In this way, we really are simple biological creatures. The wellness industry's growth is a response to our sub-or-unconscious desire to heal, whole, and prepare for the adult initiatory journey.

More healed people is a good thing, right? Yes, and the danger is that it far too often becomes a self-referential seeking. It stops at me feeling good, at me creating abundance, at my this and my that. The full arc of healing must move beyond the egocentric.

If your healing and wholing stops with you, you're only half done.

It seems that everybody wants to be the healer or the coach and few want to dig in the dirt (or however you want to describe all of the other hard, unsexy but critical work to be done). I'm not sure how to rectify this in my mind. On the one hand we need as many people as possible on the path to doing the necessary inner work. And thus we need people to lead that work. But on the other hand I see so many people swept up in the "I've got to make a career out of healing others" when it's not the best use of their talents. It's the trope of someone taking a psychedelic for the first time, having a transformative experience, and then immediately embarking on a mission to share the medicine with others. Slow down there bub.

Navigating one's own healing journey, complete with its dead ends, pitfalls, steps back, and wanderings is difficult enough. Taking a role as facilitator and guide in someone else's journey is a much more substantial responsibility. And yet it is precisely because our culture has too few true elders that the wellness industry is a net benefit. Seekers will gravitate to those that have something for them, until they don't. It's all developmental.

What the wellness community must do is evolve its understanding of what all of this healing work is for. It must ground itself back to the world and the biophysical and social realities that animate our places. Healing and wholing work must orient towards each of us arriving in True Adulthood. This is usually not an overnight process but a longer journey of preparation before embarking on your journey of soul initiation.

Unless you're fully ready for this journey, you'll sense the healing you have to do. And it'll be good work, or good enough to keep you searching and spending, inwardly focused rather than maturing to the inner work described in Part Two. And so you'll answer that niggling like we answer all nigglings in our culture: you'll spend. As David Hawkins writes in the intro to his book *Letting Go*, you'll "meditate, chant a mantra, drink green tea, try the Pentecostals, breathe in fire, and speak in tongues. You get centered, learn NLP, try actualizations, work on visualizations, study psychology, join a Jungian group. You get Rolfed, try psychedelics, get a psychic reading, jog, jazzercise, have colonics, get into nutrition and aerobics, hang upside down, wear psychic jewelry. Get more insight, bio-feedback, Gestalt therapy.

You see your homeopath, chiropractor, naturopath. You try kinesiology, discover your Enneagram type, get your meridians balanced, join a consciousness-raising group, take tranquilizers. You get some hormone shots, try cell salts, have your minerals balanced, pray, implore, and beseech. You learn astral projection. Become a vegetarian. Eat only cabbage. Try macrobiotics, go organic, eat no GMO. Meet up with Native American medicine men, do a sweat lodge. Try Chinese herbs, moxicombustion, shiatsu, acupressure, feng shui. You go to India. Find a new guru. Take off your clothes. Swim in the Ganges. Stare at the sun. Shave your head. Eat with your fingers, get really messy, shower in cold water..."

It's unlikely that a volume of ayahuasca ceremonies or meditation retreats will usher in your adulthood alone. It takes a village, one that rarely exists in modernity. It is very easy to fall into the wellness trap and support the well-intentioned spiritual economy. Remain steadfast in your understanding that your personal work must be *for* something besides yourself.

Fifteen

Soul Initiation

Reclaiming indigeneity, telling new stories, and rewriting our language are all efforts in relating to the world in a healthier, more life-sustaining way. It is a lack of relationship with all we are connected to that allows our tolerance of the abuses of overshoot and threat of existential risks. This stems from the predominant model of human relationship with the natural world: egocentrism. In the egocentric formulation, humans stand at the top of the pyramid, triumphant in their intelligence and technological prowess, with the rest of life existing to serve us, the apex species. This is juxtaposed by ecocentrism, which sees humans as part of, not above, the web life. In the ecocentric view, all species and places are essential to all other's thriving.

Soul Guide Bill Plotkin writes extensively about egocentric and ecocentric culture. He contends that approximately 80 to 90% of Western culture is made up of humans who are stuck in a state of arrested adolescence. This is because our culture fails to consistently produce true adults. True adults are ones who experience themselves in a larger context and have gone on the journey of being initiated into their particular niche of the larger ecology. This ecological niche is our soul gift, those unique talents that are part of the very fiber of our being yet are usually covered up by a culture whose values makes little room for the expression of those gifts.

In traditional cultures this journey is best facilitated through intimate partnership with nature, the spirits that animate it, and with Mystery. Under the guidance of true elders, adolescents are guided through rites of initiation in nature-based cultures that allow for one's metamorphosis into adulthood. In our culture we might get a license at 16 or the right to drink at 21 but these initiations fall far short of the deep mythic rites that stir someone at their very core inviting them into a deeper courtship of their innate gifts and personal mythos, and thus service to others.

It's hard to write a precise prescription for eco-awakening to occur. And yet once it does it opens a world of somatic, mystical, sensual, erotic, and compassionate experiences that transform one's existence. The concept of being a part of nature moves from an idea to a felt experience, a visceral, intuitive, and rooted aliveness that transforms the material world into a rich tapestry of intelligent beings worthy of our adornment, service, and cocreative attention. Once this occurs it is difficult to go back to an understanding of nature as a mere object of study or exploitation. On an individual level, the downstream results of an initiation to soul open up and restrict ways of being, doing, and consuming. If ecoawakening occurred more broadly in Western society, true adults would quickly realign our existing structures to be in service to life. What might we create when the power of our intellectual minds and technological capacity are harnessed by more whole humans? How might widespread reawakening of the many human faculties that connect us to nature change the dominant narrative?

Our cultural amnesia has us forget that we are nature herself. Our fall from grace, equivalent to us eating the apple in the Garden of Eden, is the development of our "rational thinking" — the same thinking that has allowed us to be incredible technologists, terraform the world, and rationalize all of it to keep the jig going. The developmental arc of humanity is now expanding to reintegrate that which was lost along the way. The people are awakening and reconnecting. The signs of this are everywhere.

As membership in hierarchical religious institutions and churches wanes, it is this revivification of indigeneity, an experiential reality immediately available to all, that is replacing secularism. This trend is not an accident. It is an evolutionary response to our modern world, and when integrated effectively will put the massive power of modernity in the hands of benevolent eco-centric leaders, rather than profit-maximizing ego-centric ones.

The full course of human development will always wind up in service to others, drawing from the deep inscendent well of one's true gifts to deliver what we were born to bring forward for our community. There are many ways we might offer our gift(s) and the courtship of them is a lifelong process. By "apprenticing" to these gifts and living through our personal mythos, we journey on the initiatory process to adulthood. This journey is difficult to orchestrate in modern contexts and always involves forces that are beyond human control. What appears to be true is that one must be properly prepared to go off seeking their soul. One must untangle the programming they've received, heal and whole their past traumas, and gather their internal resources enough to withstand the obliteration of ego that comes through the rebirth experienced in true rites of passage.

Rites of Passage

After some amount of personal healing work, we are ready for rites of passage which mark the passage of time and developmental progress into true adulthood.

In our society, we've left rites of initiation up to fraternities and sororities. Our cultural rites of passage are hollow, they lack the true hallmarks of an initiatory experience. True initiatory experiences are required alchemical processes on the developmental path to becoming an adult and come with significant trial, tribulation, and loss. They are documented in cultures across the world, and with good reason, as the cultures that still have healthy and functioning rites of passage have more adults than others. Our main cultural sacraments are to get a license, graduate from high school, go to college, get married, rent a car, vote, register for the draft, and be able to run for president. Most of these are rights, they are given, not earned, or earned without the necessary psycho-spiritual evolution that is the hallmark of deep initiation.

Rites of passage are vision fasts, not college binge drinking. They are dark nights of the soul, not dark nights lost in some hole. They are overwhelmingly centered in nature, in spaces that are psychologically destabilizing. They are meant to wear down your ego, chip away through the protective armor, and open the faculties to the animate world. It's more than a solo hunt in the woods or a backpacking trip. It's a dive into mythic realms and the underworld, where myth and story merge with our physical reality, spirits whisper and prod, and we die to the world we left behind. What we're ultimately seeking is the truth about ourselves, to have a run in with our own soul as reflected back by a sentient world that longs to fulfill this function.

There are many ways this rite of passage from adolescence to adulthood can take place and many ways in which a facsimile can trick us into thinking it has occurred. It could happen by quitting your job and traveling the world, or not. It could happen going to war, or not. It could happen going for a walkabout in nature, or not. Whether it happens depends on how physically, mentally, emotionally, psychologically, and spiritually prepared we are for such an experience to occur. If our culture was healthy, it would have already taught us to be in relation to our body, connected to nature and community, and capable of fully feeling and sensing. Of course most of us are not raised in a manner that cultivates these skills, nor with the proper support to regulate trauma, and as such, find that we have healing and wholing work to do before we're even ready for an initiatory experience. This journey cannot be purchased. You can buy the healing retreat or vision fast experience and never experience soul initiation. It is something you must be prepared for.

Why all this healing, wholing, and personal work as preparation? Because no matter where and when a true initiatory experience takes place it will always involve death. Our death. The death of who we once were, that adolescent identity we so carefully crafted. The ego identity that helped us be liked, fit in, succeed, and acquire wealth, status, and sex is the one that will undergo a metamorphic transformation just as the caterpillar becomes imaginal goo breaking its caterpillar body down into a mess of slimy cells. The butterfly can only emerge with wings and its full magnificence after it has completely lost all remnants of its previous form. Only then does it emerge from the cocoon in its true evolved nature. This analogy works well for our own journey. The journey of the imaginal seed of our nature, our true ecological function, must pass through the stage of full dissolution - death! - before we emerge from the goo in our true colors.

If it sounds painful, that's because it is. This journey is not without its challenges, each of ours unique, yet we all have the opportunity to go on this journey to full maturation. Absent this evolutionary journey, however it takes place, we will remain in adolescence adopting the hollow cultural rites of passage in our culture, pretending to adult by paying bills and parenting, all the while consciously or subconsciously ignoring the call within our very being to die and be reborn. Until initiated to your soul and its true calling, you will live, perhaps well off, but as a shell of what your true potential is.

Whether an initiatory journey to soul is your journey to go on, or not, developing the capabilities described throughout this book are imperative to becoming a more whole, connected human. As we heal and whole, we'll continue to increase our aptitude for somatic awareness, storytelling, sensemaking, and systems thinking. Eventually personal development at the level of our being will begin to influence our value system

Resources and Further Reading

- Soulcraft: Crossing into the Mysteries of Nature and Psyche by Bill Plotkin

- Journey of Soul Initiation by Bill Plotkin

- Nature and the Human Soul by Bill Plotkin

- Wild Mind by Bill Plotkin

- The Emerald Podcast by Joshua Schrei

- Spell of the Sensuous: Perception and Language in a More-Than-Human World by David Abram

Sixteen

New Values

I t becomes easier to understand what actions to take and *how* to take them when our system of personal values is clear. What do you value? And why? Where did those values come from? How do they serve you personally? Are they ego- or ecocentric values? Do they lead to actions and results that help us meet the challenges of our time? Or do they perpetuate it?

> **Prompt:** Look at the list of questions above and take an inventory of your values. To help you with the process, here are some categories below that may help you to decipher what you value: career, money, family/friends, things/ideas, old/new, health and wellness, leisure, spirituality, morality, creativity, community, adventure, safety, authenticity, empathy, and more.
>
> What do you see when you take stock of your values?

Values change over time. When I had just graduated from college I was brimming with ambition to take the business world by storm, a life orientation that was rooted in my belief in many of the common cultural narratives around what success looks like. I valued many of the trophies of conspicuous consumption like cars and clothes. Through the journey of personal growth, what I value has shifted from the traditional markers of success to the rich intangible experiences that pollinate the more beautiful depths of meaning.

As you increase your ability to hold the gravity of the polycrisis while improving your sensemaking capabilities and undergoing ecoawakening (no small task!), it is likely your value system will change as a natural outcome of that work. As your value system shifts, the set of possible actions also changes. This is why values are so essential. They relate to our core Why. If we understand our Why first everything else follows.

As our why takes its root in a mycelial web of connections that bind us to nature, the value system shifts from egocentric focus on ourselves to ecocentric focus on being of service to the broader world. This has been mentioned several times as an essential direction to orient to.

Once the value system begins to shift, the world becomes much easier to navigate. Soon actions that once you wouldn't have thought twice about, like buying disposable plastic or frivolous joy rides, become impossible because you understand what's really at the root of those actions and how they contribute to a world that is farther from the true desires of your now-awakened-and-connected heart. As we come to understand our place in all things, not as the center, the blossoming of our own true purpose will become the biggest bounty to our people and places.

So what might this new value system look like? Everything will begin to orient towards a life culture. You may begin to value experiences over consumption. You may begin to value that which is alive, and thus value connection with the human and non-human more. You may begin to value living well over getting ahead, placing a higher value on time and thus freedom. You may begin to value health more. You might begin to value silence and solitude more, finding richness in moments of quiet reflection rather than in constant activity and noise.

Naturally your values might differ from these. We are not copies of each other and our personal sensibilities will determine exactly how our values might shift. What's most important is that these values start to show up externally. We start to make different purchasing decisions. We stop *spending* our time in one way and start *planting* it in another. We distance ourselves from certain types of people and seek others. We begin to feed and tend our body differently. We may develop the need to slow the inexhaustible modern pace down for more nature connection time. We may start to feel more at home in our bodies, to hear it speak of its needs more clearly, and thus we begin to avoid certain artificial environments. We may begin to see how each of our actions is explicitly or covertly approving of a certain set of economic realities about the world.

Changes in values can happen slowly over time or rapidly. Shifts can happen near instantaneously or occur over the course of your development. What seems to be true is that "once you open the door you can't go back." The shift from *ego*centric to *eco*centric appears to be irreversible. Once the relational landscape has been remapped in a way that opens our heart to the true nature of life and our place in it, it cannot be undone.

We Made It All Up

The shift in personal context allows us to see the world in new ways. As new capacities open up within us and a new more grounded value system takes hold, what once was is now seen in a different light. The highway and stop lights have not physically changed. And yet it soon seems less like "the way it always was" as we remember the land from the perspective of the land. When we awaken the dream of the earth within us we begin to see that everything around us - the buildings, infrastructure, organizations, businesses, busy-ness, cell phones, schools, vehicles, houses, economy, culture - we made it all up. We. Made. It. All. Up. That the structures and systems that define our entire lives are inventions of human imagination. None of it existed before it did. Some man or woman somewhere decided that this is the way it will be. And now it is.

As our perspective becomes more ecological we begin to feel time differently. We open up to long time, to the songs of our ancestors over thousands of years. To the changes that take millennia, not two quarters and a bonus from now. We become the lens of the satellite camera that for the first time glimpsed our entire planet in the famous Pale Blue Dot photo: our context expands massively. What used to matter shrinks. It's as if...none of this were even real. All the rules and creation. The whole frame of what we rush around in every day. It's like we made it all up. Because we did. It's all a dream.

There are many spiritual traditions that hold that this reality is all a dream. The Vedic and Buddhist traditions call it the maya, the world of illusory appearances. The Hermetic wisdom tradition from Egypt holds that all is in the mind. Shamans the world over say that we are all just dreaming.

If all beings are dreaming, does that mean that Earth is dreaming? If we are the dream of the earth, what dream does it have for itself? Is nature its dream? What does it dream for us? Are we the manifestation of the Earth's dream? Or its nightmare? Are our dreams ours? Or does the Earth dream through us? If we attune our senses, can we hear and see the Earth's dream? Perhaps we've been coaxed by marketing and our trauma to chase the wrong dream? Perhaps we're tuned into the wrong signal?

Would the earth dream a dream that was self-destructive for our species? For itself? Or does it dream of the highest potential inherent within our capability? If it is dreaming right now, what would it take for us to awaken to that dream?

What If...There's Nothing Wrong?!

If we are really part of Earth's dream, then there is a question that must be considered: What if there's nothing wrong?

What if the entire polycrisis, all the many man-made systems and structures and realities that are worth lamenting over, what if there's nothing wrong? What if all of this - the wars, famine, poverty, inequality, hatred, politics, overshoot - what if it's all part of some greater plan by Gaia herself? Perhaps this is all just the arc of evolution....

In nature it's been observed over and over again how populations of species become so successful that they overshoot their resource base and collapse. This has been observed in the moose of Isle Royale, locusts in Asia and Africa, penguins in Antarctica, and moths in North America. If overshoot is the nature of life on this planet, and because we are in fact part of nature, not above it, why preclude ourselves from the possibility of humanity's overshoot? Our population is ballooning, we are overusing resources, and soon we might collapse. Is it so out of the question? Might it not be wrong?

From the Mayans and Anasazi to the Khmer and Easter Island, history is littered with examples of civilizations that mysteriously disappeared with little explanation. Perhaps all of the lost civilizations were just earlier versions of this same pattern playing out. Using our pattern recognition skills we can begin to see a cycle in human history of human populations rapidly declining after substantial growth, albeit on a more localized scale. The difference now is the global scale of our civilization which binds us together as one.

This question is worth wrestling with. What if there's nothing wrong? What are the implications of this? What might be true if all of the reasons why we lament our current situation are the natural course of evolution?

What's different now, we hope, is that general human intelligence and capability is higher than it ever was in the past. Meaning that if our species is indeed going through a great initiation in the form of impending collapse, we have an enhanced ability to find the gift for our species in the wounds we will bear. These wounds will require not just psychospiritual adjustment but the rearranging of our physical world as well.

Centuries ago when we deprioritized the cultural knowledge we had been creating for many generations of how to be intimately connected with our world, overshoot and collapse may have become the inevitable result. Our retreat from nature into the gilded (c)age of capitalism brought us advances that were once only the playthings of sci-fi writers. Now that we've actualized such "progress" the next step of our evolution is to again return to the lifemaker, Earth, with a new, more complete species skill set that will unlock the true potential of our generativity. Imagine our power harnessed in ways that fully partner with ecology, at first out of necessity, a forcing function of biological limits, and ultimately out of the arrival of our hearts back in communion with the animate world around us that cheers our return as a wiser and more responsible cohabitor of Earth.

Giving up the interpretation that there's something wrong requires us to hold lightly to our sensemaking about this moment in time. Though our science and reason suggests cause for concern, who am I, or you, or people twice as smart as us to believe we have the correct understanding of what is playing out on generational scales? Our purview is the past but certainly not the future. As cosmic forces play out the grand drama through us at greater time scales, perhaps what is needed on our behalf is Trust. Beyond fear of what might happen is a state of trust that "everything is working out exactly as it should". This is a type of surrender, an acknowledgement that we are but lone agents in the most complex orchestration we know.

Doomerism and existential dread would have us concede that all is already lost. "Haven't you grasped the severity of the situation?!" they ask. "We are rearranging deck chairs on the Titanic" they'll quip. "Don't you see the signs everywhere? Eight degrees of warming is "baked in'". There's no point. Why bother? All is lost. Or if it isn't all lost, that our actions are futile against forces beyond our control. This might be true. Hopefully you've already sat with this. All might be lost with inevitable collapse on the horizon. And...what if that isn't wrong? Perhaps it is the very moment of our greatest triumph when we as a species come full circle to a balanced way of existing in harmony with each other and the planet.

Just because there's nothing wrong, doesn't mean that we eschew our responsibility, cop out to inaction, and passively watch the play unfold. Meeting the Moment is first about arriving at the truth by developing the skills necessary to evaluate, make sense of, and feel what appears to be true. Shedding the interpretation that there's something wrong can then empower us towards action. It is the realization that we can only go from here. Each of us is helping to decide our collective destination. It is the clarion call for us to take up our craft and true service as developmental agents of Earth's evolutionary dream seeking to play itself out through us.

Prompt: What freedom lies beyond the interpretation that something is wrong? Who then might we be free *to be*? What shackles of our choosing might we unchain if we allow ourselves the affordance of hope? Journal on the consideration that despite everything we've covered, there is, in fact, nothing wrong.

Seventeen

Hope and Choice

Beyond Hope

H ope is among the most complicated of human states of being. It can slingshot us to unbelievably great outcomes or lock us into mind-boggling failures and self-delusional fantasies. Amidst our challenging reality, is there cause for hope? Can hope be healthy? And if so, how?

By definition, hope is a belief in some future that is not present, and perhaps unlikely to be present. It is both a feeling and a thought pattern. Hope is part inspiration, part prayer. Like all things, it has both negative and positive aspects. The negative pole of hope is fantasy. It's the mode of being that allows us to believe that technology will be our total savior. That if we just science a little harder we'll figure out some solution. That somehow the gordian knot will untangle itself. That someone out there is working on *the* solution right now.

Hope can easily slide into unjustified hope. False hope anchors our beliefs to outcomes that verge towards the horrendously unreasonable. Some would argue the purpose of hope is to stretch us beyond all reasonable limits. But false hope is a setup for failure and disappointment because it is *too ungrounded* and removed from current reality. It opens us up to magical thinking, which itself is useful in spiriting our imagination, but can also leave us susceptible to pure fantasy outside of the realm of possibility.

Is it reasonable to bet the future of our species and planet on false hope? What is the right amount of hope? Should we hope for air scrubbers to remove CO_2? Should we hope for a solution to the climate aspect of the polycrisis? And that the climate solutions will buy us enough time for everything else to be solved?

More importantly, how can hope exist in a person who at the same time has come to grips with the stark realities of our situation? How can we maintain hope amidst the daily barrage of news? An often-cited and well-researched story comes from Admiral Stockdale who was captured in Korea as a prisoner of war. He said that "you must never confuse faith that you will prevail in the end—which you can never afford to lose—with the discipline to confront the most brutal facts of your current reality, whatever they might be." He noted that it was those that hoped, without acknowledging the brutal facts of reality, that often didn't make it out of the prisoner camps because it was their hope that was dashed over and over again which ultimately broke their spirits. The trick is to both hope, and be as realistic as possible, and hold the two at the same time. We must live the both/and.

To those that observe and make sense of the world, there is little cause for hope. Geopolitically, socially, economically, educationally, and of course ecologically, there is plenty of information to suggest that the global situation is in fact hopeless. And so in the face of all the forces and trends that seem immoveable, tying the gordian knot even tighter, hope is in fact a choice that requires courage. There's a bravado to staring into the abyss and still believing that we'll make it out, scathed to be sure, yet triumphant as a species.

We must hope. In the essential movie *The Matrix*, the Architect says that "Hope, it is the quintessential human delusion, simultaneously the source of your greatest strength, and your greatest weakness." The strength comes from our ability to anchor a vision of what we know is possible, as told by our new stories. This hope, when grounded into our somatically-awakened, emotionally-in-tuned, developmentally-progressed, whole-and-healed Self, becomes the purest bell ringing amidst the modern calamity, a courageous cry for "the more beautiful world our heart's know is possible" that stokes the fire of Will and breeds determination in the face of potential futility.

And yet hope's weakness is living as if the fantasy were actually coming true, blinding us to the contradicting realities that would render our hope fruitless. If we are to Meet the Moment, we must simultaneously hope and move beyond hope too. As Admiral Stockdale did, we must acknowledge that in the worst of projected scenarios there is no cause for hope. We'll never make it out of the prison camp. Depressing, yes. But we have the body to hold that emotion. We've built the self-awareness to process it. We're connected to the land to go give our grief to. So there's no hope, now what?

Towards Choice

Hope alone will not suffice because the situation is also beyond hope. That leaves us with us choice. Pesky, beguiling choice. It's all we have.

Our lives are mostly made up of our time and the series of choices that we make in that time. Choice is our agency and the greatest power we have. The more privilege we have, the greater the range of choices available to us. We get to choose what and how much we buy, where we live and why, who we vote for, how much we participate in the system, who we converse with about what, and on and on and on. We choose how actively we pursue our healing, how far we're willing to go developmentally, how we want to be, what we choose to be relation to, how we cultivate that relationship, what we think about our moment, and just what in the hell we're actually going to *do* about all this.

As we increase our sovereignty and break the ties of cultural, social, and political programming, we grow our meta-skills around how we make our choices. Now we can assess who is making the choice? As in, from what part in myself am I making this choice? What am I trying to accomplish? What unmet need am I seeking to meet? Is that need life-generative, or life-denying, for me? Is that need life-generative, or life-denying, for the world? Have I separated out need from want? To what am I in service to?

> **Practice: Discernment**, that skill of understanding what's true, pointed inward with Self-Awareness, married in the context of our Values, is how we effectively ask and answer important questions in a manner that helps us to best Meet the Moment ethically and honorably.

As we consider our choices, we must also keep in mind the concept of Sphere of Control. Originating back to the time of the Stoic philosophers and popularized by Stephen Covey in his important book *The 7 Habits of Highly Effective People*, the Sphere of Control is a model that helps us perceive what is and isn't within the realm of us having an effect on it. Pictured here, it invites us to consider what we have control over, what we might influence, and what concerns us but is neither in our influence or control.

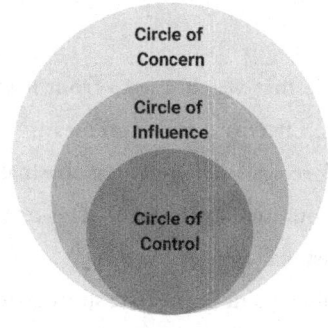

Sphere of Control

The Sphere of Control reminds us to focus on that which we can do something about. Too often we attempt to focus on and waste precious time and attention on the Circle of Concern. If we are to make the most of our choices we must focus on that which we can control. This speaks to our original theory of change, that by focusing first on what we can most control, *our being*, we'll have a greater influence over *our doing*, and thus over what we can influence.

Different people can populate their circles with different items. The more egocentric we are, the less likely we are to perceive the many dynamics of our current global moment and place them in our Circle of Concern. To the ecocentric individual, our Circle of Concern is the whole globe, all of its inhabitants, and everything interconnected to both. As we expand our systems thinking we begin to see how different elements of our world are nested within each other, and thus how action and influence fractal up and down. Rivers are nested within watersheds nested in bioregions. Cities are nested within states nested within countries. Teams are nested within companies nested within markets. Our choices at one level can affect the other. Through the Sphere of Control, we must practice our both/and thinking, keeping in heart and mind our Circle of Concern connected to all life, while also being realistic about what we can Control and Influence.

Whether we hope, or we don't, or both, everything comes to reality when we make our choices. From the smallest choice, what toothpaste we use in the morning, to the largest choice, where we live and why and how, each choice is helping create the world that is becoming. Many of the impacts of our choices are not obvious. When we buy junk plastic items, it's not apparent at the cash register the entire resource-intensive process that brings that item to us. When we buy fast fashion, it's not apparent that there's human labor toiling for barely passable wages somewhere on the other side of the world. As our connection grows we become more aware of the manufacturing and transportation costs hidden upstream from our lifestyle choices. Beneficial choices are the outcome of our sensemaking, values, and expanding relationality.

Time Discounting

In the looming shadow of the polycrisis, it is preferable that we choose to front load choices today that in the future will be forced upon us. Effective adaptation means we make changes *before* they are necessary. The human track record on doing this is abysmal. We are chronically hindered by one of our greatest flaws: our inability to act on long-term thinking. This is a problem of what behavioral economists call *time discounting*.

Time discounting refers to the tendency of individuals to value immediate short-term gratifications more highly than long-term future benefits, leading to a preference for receiving benefits in the present rather than in the future. This phenomenon explains why people might choose a smaller, immediate payoff over a larger, delayed one, illustrating how perceived value diminishes as the delay to receiving a reward increases. Time discounting underlies many decisions and behaviors, affecting financial planning, health-related choices, and general impulsivity.

Time discounting explains the gap between what we know we should do – make hard challenging decisions and sacrifices to stem overshoot — from what we actually do — kick the can down the road and rationalize that reality away. Because we seem broadly incapable of choosing later over now, it is often crisis that forces us to finally take the actions that were obvious many months, years, or decades in the past. The squeaky wheel does indeed get the grease, or perhaps, the loudest crisis gets the least we'll sacrifice. It doesn't have to be this way. So it shouldn't surprise you that it is adolescents who are the ones primarily incapable of sacrificing for the future. To overcome both our evolutionary propensity for instant gratification and modern culture's economic offerings, we can try the following:

- Invest more time discerning needs from wants, thick from thin desires

- Consider all actions in relation to your values. We often sacrifice long-term ideals for short-term gratification. Anchor the *why* behind any sacrifices you deem necessary. There's no reason to be a martyr, and also some outcomes require you to give a little now for a different outcome later. Understand that sacrificing is a gamble – sure, it might not pay off. But what if it does? Then you'll be the person who lived your values to the ends you dreamed possible.

- Remember that everything gets easier over time. Get the ball rolling and notice how choices build momentum in your habits and actions over time.

The Four Horsemen of Personal Responsibility

So why don't we do more? It's not like much of what we've covered about how our modern world works is new news. Why don't we act? Either at the behest of our professed religion's scripture, the empathy we feel, or even self-interest?

In addressing ecological overshoot it seems that we fall victim to a set of logical fallacies that allow us to maintain business-as-usual. These logical errors in our thinking are pervasive and tricky to address. The Four Horsemen of Personal Responsibility are Rationalization, Scapegoating, Doomism, and Naive Optimism. Together and in any combination they create a psychological wall that ensures most of our attention on the polycrisis fails to translate into choice and action, with cognitive dissonance and other coping strategies taking their place.

Horseman One: I'm Just A Drop in the Bucket

If I don't do it someone else will. Do you really think that if I stop doing X that it will make a difference when there are a billion other people doing the same thing? I've heard it a hundred times. I've even used it myself to justify some of my own past behaviors. The logic seems sound from the outside. The math adds up. I can't possibly make a difference in the equation. Comparing my tiny impact to a larger whole is the easiest way to minimize my own culpability. I'm just a drop in the bucket.

Adopting this rationalization punches a ticket to endlessly continuing the behavior in question. The fallacy of the argument is that everyone thinks the same thing. There is no full bucket without each individual drop, so even the most obvious actions that seem unnecessary, like buying fast fashion or using single-use plastics, become justifiable. Part of the challenge is the first mover disadvantage. It pays to be a first mover on a hot stock, when you're trying to get more privilege, but it pays not to be an early mover when giving up a behavior. Why go first? The first Horsemen is close friends with the second...

Horseman Two: It's Their Fault

They make it available. They produce it. Blame the big guys. They should know us little guys are going to buy it and use it so they bear the responsibility to stop. Don't blame the demand side of the equation, blame the supply. This is Scapegoating, the second Horseman which is an expert at passing the blame. While Rationalization passes the blame to an amorphous collective, "the bucket", Scapegoating passes it off to some place in particular, usually the big bad corporation.

But wait, it's not the corporations. Blame the lobbyists. Blame the corrupt politicians. One and two work hand-in-hand. One minimizes our part in it all and two passes the blame on. Together they ensure that the personal culpability we have for our decisions is reduced below a level that we find tolerable enough to continue our behaviors. And then it's back to out-of-sight out-of-mind. Because we already know it's really easier not to think about it all. And why ruin an otherwise perfectly good day?

Horseman Three: It's too late

The third horseman arrives in sentiments like "it's too late", "it doesn't matter anyway", and "our fate was sealed a long time ago". This perspective encourages us to fully surrender to a fate that is already sealed. Action is futile in the face of an all-but-certain fate.

The more depressing end of this spectrum becomes doomerism, people who are convinced and obsessed with our inevitable demise. True doomers don't even bother prepping. They take no action at all because "it won't matter, we'll all die anyway." While many people don't slide as far as full doomers, they adopt an attitude that "what's going to happen is going to happen with or without me". This horseman would prefer that you remain absent any hope or motivation to take action. Why bother?

Horseman Four: "Earth Will Be Fine"

The fourth horsemen however prefers your hope with sentiments like "earth will be fine, it's humans who have to worry" and "I'm sure we'll invent some technology for that". This is Naive Optimism where abject faith is placed in it all working out. The spiritual-based person might even note that it can't be any other way than it is. This pollyanna perspective puts so much blind faith in everything being okay that it prefers not to acknowledge less-than-rosy outcomes in the set of possible future outcomes. And so because "everything will work out" it becomes another crafty mental method of ensuring that personal behavior doesn't have to change.

An honorable mention should go to "I'll just move off grid" as if somehow a stockpile of goods and just a bit of distance will isolate and protect someone from serious collapse. For every billionaire building their lavish end-of-the-world bunker, of which there are many, it's laughable to think of this as a truly viable solution. What good is a world without a healthy ecology and people?

The Horsemen are the most pervasive mental shenanigans we play to ensure as little as possible disruption to our personal lives. They are of course an incomplete list of the ways we rationalize and explain away personal responsibility for our current situation. If we are to Meet the Moment we must take careful stock of the rationalizations and mental tricks we employ to justify our behavior, or lack thereof.

Inaction is Action Too

"He who passively accepts evil is as much involved in it as he who helps to perpetrate it. He who accepts evil without protesting against it is really cooperating with it."

Dr. Martin Luther King, Jr.

The easiest action is often no action. It requires no extra effort. It doesn't ask us to stop and think, to consider deeply, to take time away from our task at hand. Inaction is acceptance. It is explicitly saying, what's happening is okay with me. Inaction is indifference. It declares that what's occurring is not important enough for me to care one way or the other.

No choice is still a choice.

Inaction has witnessed great tragedies. People whose inaction leads them to lament that "if only I had just done XYZ, then..." It has allowed what was easily preventable to occur. It has tacitly endorsed violence. It has abandoned higher potential to the devious designs of the greedy. Inaction is the means by which the dynamics of the polycrisis stay stuck. If I do nothing, perhaps it at least won't get worse. As humans, we often develop a tendency to avoid change, as it is always change that brings the "bad". Though of course it is change that also always precedes "good", it seems we develop a stronger dislike of the bad than a like of the good. Evolutionary psychologists suspect this might be an adaptive measure that is oriented towards our survival. The irony of this psychological mechanism is that it might actually be encouraging us to defer action when we need it most.

What's Worth Doing Anyway?

Switching contexts and playing devil's advocate helps us test our thinking and conclusions and allows us to assess if there are actions we can take right now that make sense regardless of the context we find ourselves in. Let's assume for a minute that the entire pretense of the polycrisis is false. It's highly likely it isn't. But what if it is? What if there is no overshoot, resource crunch, climate change, geopolitical strife, etc... Then what? What if the core assumptions of this book are inaccurate?

What's worth doing anyway? What's worth doing if the seas don't rise and global food shortages don't happen and wars over resources don't erupt and the economic house of cards never falls? What's worth doing anyway with our one wild and precious life? What has merit on its own accord? If we've cultivated our skills to Meet the Moment, the answers to these questions look remarkably similar regardless of our context.

Would an eco-awakened human return to mindless consumption if it was announced with 100% confidence "just kidding the hundred years of science is wrong"? Someone who feels their Indigeneity through the relational bonds between themselves, the land, their ancestors, and the more-than-human world, would they allow the destruction of the local habitat? Would someone who's healed-and-wholed on the journey to understanding the true gift of their ecological niche tolerate a culture that keeps the true initiatory rites hidden from its youth in favor of creating good consumers? No.

When what we value changes, choice and outcomes follow necessarily.

By first addressing our individual requirements for personal development, the solutions begin to become self-evident. When what we value changes, choice and outcomes follow necessarily. Our adolescent culture values the classic fantasy of money, power, and status. This reality is the basis of the all-too-common midlife crisis. Someone has chased these cultural trophies and either acquired them, or not, but either way feels of their hollowness. Realizing life's half over, the midlifer begins to consider their legacy amidst the realization of how short life really is. Maybe they do something impactful with their crisis, maybe not.

The kicker is that a mid-life crisis is completely avoidable by doing the developmental work that puts us on the path to true adulthood. As it turns out, most of the endeavors that people wind up engaging in during retirement, or if money becomes no object, are the life-generating actions that don't require money, power, or status to enjoy. Substantial research shows that among the most satisfying actions we can take is being of service to others rather than self. It's not just easier to skip all the lusting after our cultural gold; it's necessary to reduce the consumption driving the economic system. The sooner each of us "unplugs from the matrix" the quicker it becomes apparent what's actually meaningful. It will always circle back to life in some form. It will inevitably circle back to the intangibles that make human life beautiful. Hospice and death workers report that people on their deathbed do not wish they earned or spent more money, or worked or accomplished more, but that they had spent more time with loved ones, taken more risks, and lived more richly and deeply into the moments now gone.

Regardless of what's true about our current situation, the purpose of life, of all life, is to continue itself. The late-stage terminal capitalism we find ourselves trapped in is antithetical to the continuance of life. **Even if all of the assumptions around our many crises are false, despite what appears to be true, what's worth doing anyway is that which serves life and brings about greater health and evolution.**

Sensemaking suggests it's unlikely the polycrisis is predominantly false. It seems the boat is sinking. So if we know it's going down, do we party? Is it time for hedonism? Shall we shovel the coal of consumption into the engine more quickly and send the boat hurtling towards the icebergs we know are ahead? Is this the world you want to build?

Or does it seem like in the face of all the doom there's cause to choose active hope? To acknowledge the boat is sinking and take action to slow or even reverse the demise because doing so requires us to engage in whole sets of behaviors that affirm life, generate health, increase our relationships, deepen our humanity, get us in touch with our full capabilities, stretch us beyond our current ableness, and bring us into alignment with the true gifts stowed within our life vessel?

We have a choice of what kind of world we want to live in. Even *if* we are able to innovate our way out of this mess, to suck all of the carbon out of the air, reverse global warming, mine asteroids to solve all of our resource issues, deploy AI to solve our problems, and thus keep the global engine of economics charging full speed ahead, do you want to live where that future is going? Where inequality is more extreme? Where we are a multi-planet species further segmenting off the haves and have-nots? Where more of our people continue down the path as adolescent consumers rather than stepping into true ecoawakened adulthood?

Eighteen

Enoughness

How much is enough? When I was a teenager I wanted more. More cars. More clothes. More women. Society models more is the way. I remember a counselor once told me I was living in a world of grandiosity. I pitied him and his small life. I was going to have it all. And so I set off into the world to do so, half-heartedly, always feeling the journey of this book tug at my heart as my income, possessions, and lifestyle increased. I, too, found myself on the treadmill of having more, wanting more, and striving for that. How much is enough? Always a little more!

Our world is awash with marketing hammering home the concept that we are not enough, but might be, if we just had the newest [insert product/service here]. The entire economic system is driven by not enoughness. That is why everything is measured in growth. Gross Domestic Product must go up at all costs. The only enough is more.

The wound of enoughness permeates the human experience and replicates itself across generations and relationships. Somewhere along the way we likely receive the programming that "you aren't enough." It often comes from a parent, teacher, or partner. The typical responses are either a.) taking on that we're not enough and living into that by being smaller in the world or b.) doing everything possible to compensate for that perceived lack by proving just how much we actually are. These strategies can play out over entire careers and lifetimes without people recognizing that's what they're doing. Our culture's external orientation leads to our proving enoughness through all manners of external accumulation.

And yet nothing we seek outside ourselves will fill a perceived gap within us because that gap is not fillable with status, possessions, power, sex – you name it, it will never fully satisfy. And if it seems to, it is a temporary illusion we have crafted for ourselves. Because the truth is that there are no gaps within us. We have always been enough. We are not broken or incomplete. There's no smallness to shrink to, no bigness we must strive for. We are born whole and complete, worthy, and already enough in our potential. This is the internal mission that can't be completed by seeking out there. We sure do try though. How much has happened in the world because a man's relationship with the size of his lower member subconsciously drove him to compensate for his *perceived* lack of enoughness? How often do we idolize the conspicuous consumption of celebrities? How much do we feed the funnels of lifestyle influencers with likes and purchases of their sponsored merch?

If I just get all of that, *then* I'll be happy.

Which is rubbish.

The correlation between financial independence and happiness is well documented to be weak at best. Having more money (external enoughness) does not predict someone's level of happiness (beyond a certain lower threshold). That this is the typical conversation is the problem to begin with. We've mistaken the goal to be happiness. What's the problem with happiness? It's too often associated with ease and convenience. If you optimize for happiness you will most likely stay within your comfort zone where you will grow less than by challenging yourself to your full potential.

In a world where materialism and peak experiences are social media statements, the real brags aren't found scrolling on a digital feed but in the privacy of our own offline lives and in our analog hearts. Opposite conspicuous consumption and the incremental ascension of luxury and status, the real flexes are being healthy, having your precious time, taking responsibility for one's self, showing up to Meet the Moment, and being in deep connection with the human-and-more-than-human world. This is the type of abundance one wouldn't bother to quantify on a dashboard because measurement will always fail to capture the essence of its true value in our lives. The new "cool" is unplugging yourself from the matrix, moving towards self-sustainability, and meeting your needs in ways many don't.

When you've become enough, on the inside, the external needs for enoughness decrease significantly. As I've gone on this journey, I've witnessed my consumption decrease because I'm no longer making purchases in order to project some meme or self-value into the world. I'm less interested in the clothes we wear or the cars we drive. I find that fewer of my actions are compensatory, meaning they are not with the purpose of earning something from you, whether it's acceptance, love, belonging, connection, etc... because I am actively cultivating these qualities in and for myself.

The truth is we don't need as much as we're told we do. We can be happy with less. A lot less. Paradoxically having less can actually lead to a richer and more fulfilling life. A life filled with connection over endless striving. One investing time in building that which is life-affirming instead of contributing to ecocide. A way of being that unlocks the full potential of our humanity instead of being living replicators of adolescent memes.

At some point in the maturation process it becomes apparent how much enough is and why. This is not a decision but a feeling that arises from a connecting with Self that derives satisfaction from within rather than outside. There is tremendous freedom in stepping off of the hedonic treadmill, the aptly named metaphor for our consumption society which like a treadmill propels us forward towards the next breadcrumb of a purchase. It seems one of the only ways out of our current world predicament is for more people to Want Less, Buy Less, and Use Less. We must eagerly seek all the ways enoughness is found within ourselves, complete with the succulent intangibles of life that decorate the rich relational existence of our being.

Adherents to manifestation culture, abundance mindset, The Secret, and prosperity gospel may find the concept of less repulsive and a denial of our inalienable right to abundance. Each takes the reality that *we do live on an abundant planet* and translates that into a narrative that our inherent internal worth is only fully actualized by an external cornucopia of wealth. "As within, so without", "God wills abundance in your life" they say. Both the New Age and Christianity have been corrupted by capitalism using "abundance" as a spiritual justification for consumerism. This stamp of approval ensures participation in the business-as-usual rat race while stealthily reinforcing narratives about enoughness being achieved through external means. This completely ignores realities about the finiteness of resources and the spiritual responsibility of ecological stewardship present in all traditions if you excavate beneath the deposited layers of propagandized popular culture.

The paradigm shifts when one discovers the capability to find true happiness without more than the bare essentials. Yes, nestled in each day, within ourselves, is all we could ever need. Beyond striving. Beyond incompleteness. The fulfillment of our lives exists in Meeting the Moment, the very moment where in gratitude you breathe and feel the contentment of your own enoughness already independent of those external agendas that seek to motivate your action towards some innocuous direction.

Prompt: Think about your purchases over the last three months. Journal about why you made the purchases. Were they because of a genuine need? How many were because of a desire? What identity were you reinforcing? What is it you were really seeking? How might you find what you were seeking within yourself?

The journey to enoughness unlocks a deeper discernment between wants and needs. As the internal motivators of desire become more apparent to your self-observation, it becomes easier to spot which desires are thick, originating from true need, and which are thin, arising from false wants. Wants unneccessarily become needs because they help to bring psycho-emotional safety and security to identity. The more we rely on the latest flavor of striving as a proxy for us being enough the more we will confuse wants with needs.

Being enough is the path to freedom and personal sovereignty. It is in feeling complete, whole, and enough that we are to fully arrive. Arriving is not such an easy thing. To really arrive is to finally land in the moment present to all the internal murmuring and external screams plying for your attention, begging action, and despite the awareness of this never-ending parade not feel pulled in any specific direction because you no longer feel compelled to compensate, strive, achieve, prove, or meet expectations. Contrary to suspicions that this is an empty state devoid of meaning, these are the moments in which you feel your Self, unique in form and essence, as truly enough. Beyond the need to impress, supplanting the agenda of marketeers and gurus, integrating all the wound-gifts that emerge along the journey, the discovery of enoughness frees us from the shackles of our own protective strategies into the eminence of our worth.

In a world that screams more is better, enough is best.

We All Can't Be the HBIC

I know. You want to have your own thing. It makes for a great story at Thanksgiving. Mom will be impressed. Your friends will laud you on social media. You want to be up to something. And what better way than to start your own modality, training, business, coaching practice, online course, or content.

Let's be honest. Being the boss is nice. So is making the schedule and the rules. Sure all the pressure and problems are your ultimate responsibility but when you succeed you can tell of your triumph, your dogged entrepreneurial spirit that speaks of your worthiness, determination, and cleverness. Particularly now with your new values that are contextually appropriate for the Moment.

But what if, brace yourself, the best way you can contribute is to support someone else's thing. Oh the terror! How ambition recoils. "How will I make a name for myself?!" ego retorts. The reality is that there are so many solutions to the challenges of our time, some old, some new. And what many of these worthwhile and beneficial ideas need is not another competitor to splinter our attention and power, they need more support, willpower, and heart.

"Too many chiefs not enough Indians", or "too many cooks in the kitchen", does not serve us. We need to mobilize. And so before creating the next permutation of what's already been done, are we asking ourselves if this new thing is, with our name on the front, really necessary? Many leaders shouldn't be in leadership but they are because of our obsession with status and income. Being the boss is often just a proxy for "make more money." If your wants and needs are less because you've stepped off the hedonic treadmill, would being the boss be necessary or desirable? If you've done the ego work to not have it all be about you, do you need to be out front? What is really the right role and lane for your incredible talents?

Nineteen

Justice

The arc of the moral universe is long, but it bends toward justice."

Martin Luther King

Human history chronicles the rise and fall of ideas and empires and the inevitable march of progress throughout the ages. It is a story that heralds winners and losers and the many consequences of those triumphs and failures. It is easy to see that human behavior throughout history is often neither just or equitable. Modern history is particularly full of the many struggles to balance the scales between those that have wealth, rights, power, and access and those that don't.

Today the scales remain grossly imbalanced. While significant progress has been made advancing human rights, these hard fought battles do not guarantee that the advances are secure. There are people and ideologies who at this very moment are plotting how to regain power and control over those who have seen their wealth, power, access, or rights expand.

What is justice in the context of the polycrisis? In a culture that is transitioning from egocentrism to ecocentrism, justice would result in outcomes that are more equitable and evenly distributed. The struggles and campaigns to address poverty, racism, and women's rights are virtuous and absolute necessities to bring harmony and balance to our man-made and natural systems. Yet there is a real danger in devoting such significant resources to outcomes that will still be nested within an unhealthy system. Alleviating poverty by increasing spending power to welcome the poor and Global South into consumerism will not lead to systemic or cultural health. Eliminating racism so that everyone can compete fairly in the zero-sum competition of corporate chutes-and-ladders will only reinforce the structures that be. If we're not careful, feminism will simply feed the hydra of tops-down decision making and erode the many, beautiful differences between the genders that nourish life and healthy community.

That the many social justice issues are systemic is the result of who has dominated the systems for decades and centuries. As easy as it is for some to point at white males, a more accurate view is the adolescents who have created the rules by which the game is played. Arriving in true adulthood unlocks compassion, empathy, connection, and mutual respect, personality characteristics that acknowledge the fundamental, inalienable rights of life that each of us are endowed with. The tensions of social justice have become the front lines for culture wars that conveniently distract us from the larger context of capitalism relentlessly profiting in the background as it undermines (literally and figuratively) the natural systems that support all life.

Nature is color blind. It does not see 2SLGBTQIA+. It does not see race, religion, creed, sexual orientation, or any of the other protected classes. It is bound by energy, metabolism, and system dynamics. Unlike plagues in the Bible, hurricanes, floods, and fires do not discriminate. Which is only half-true because it is typically the underprivileged who find themselves in the direct path of disaster and who are less able to absorb the shock. Yet nature is fundamentally the original equal opportunity employer. It offers equally to every human a connection whose riches are the ecoawakening previously described.

It's sad that vying for a just and equitable world is a contentious position today. For those whose enoughness is derived from havingness and power, the tides of justice whose cries forever lap the shore of human culture are an existential threat to egocentrism. The power of a return to the land, to recentering ecology, is that while access to higher education and capital can be constrained, the evocative intimacy of a deep relationship with nature cannot. It's right outside the front door inviting disillusionment with the current system, a rejection of its promises, and a blossoming of life cultures whose people, projects, and behaviors will reshape the future.

There are millions who have neither the time nor capacity to engage in Meeting the Moment because the system has already failed them. This is an injustice which can only be rectified by all of us living up to the responsibility of privilege. There are those whose fingers more substantially tip the scales economically, environmentally, and socially. They are the 1% and the 10% who are disproportionately responsible for global consumption. The "leaders" who fail to consider the entire web of consequence from their decisions.

The media and pop culture goliaths who sway many people with their mimetic creations. Equality, equity, and justice could emerge in all of these instances as a result of the grander reorientation to life that occurs in the passage from egocentric pathology to ecocentric maturity. As long as social justice warriors engage at the fault lines of fragile egos and identities wrapped around the past and the status quo, we will fail to reconcile these tensions to a higher order of human cooperation.

Advancing societies that are bioregional, ecologically-grounded, and sustainable will meet the true needs of humans in a way that brings about more justice and equity. In part three, we'll Come Together and explore how we might actualize this reality.

Privilege

What is the essence of privilege? By definition, privilege is a special right or advantage which is granted or available to only a particular person or group. For those who have it, it can be difficult to see. For those that don't, its absence is painfully present. It has the power to completely shape our worldview and the difference in the lifestyle, access, and treatment between those who have it and those who don't is astoundingly significant.

Privilege comes in many forms. Peggy McIntosh lists "sexual orientation, employment, class, physical ability, region, handedness, religion, language, nation of origin, gender, gender identity, ethnicity, a families' relation to money, education, housing, neighborhoods, and a families' languages of origin" as some of the domains in which privilege exists.

It can be difficult to see from the inside. For those that grow up with some type of privilege, or have grown accustomed to it, life becomes normal from that particular advantage point. Access to quality education or the presumption of innocence are very different depending on the socio-economic background one comes from. When you're surrounded by others with similar privilege it becomes the social norm. Normative ways of being and acting emerge during childhood and are impactful on shaping human identity. Soon privilege can become an entitlement, a projected expectation that privilege be maintained.

Privilege is self-reinforcing. It congregates with other privileges and builds momentum to maintain itself. As is said, birds of a feather. And when called out, privilege often uses a myriad of explanations to justify itself. Social Darwinism, "it's a stroke of luck", recounting the scoreboard of past compensatory actions, pointing to the positive outcomes i.e.

"the ends justify the means", or trickle-down economics are a few of the many defense mechanisms consciously or subconsciously deployed.

Humans like privileges. They're alluring and externally validate the internal feelings of specialness that most possess. People like to sit in the private box at sports parks and have access to the faster moving line. This validation makes it feel like we deserve to be where we are. Our velvet rope society caters to this perfectly for a cost. And it seems that when those who are disadvantaged quickly gain privilege they accept it readily as if it's due to them rather than breaking a cycle of haves and have nots. *The Dictator's Handbook* describes in detail the truth behind the classic aphorism "one man's terrorist is another man's freedom fighter." Examples abound from Africa and South America of how quickly the deprived liberators become the privileged oppressors. Similarly, in the Stanford prison experiment, access to privilege was purposefully manipulated and both the guards and prisoners eagerly played into their new found privilege to shocking results. In many political coups, the formerly downtrodden faction which usurps power is intoxicated with their new authority and quickly become the brutalizers they despise.

Privilege's existence is tightly interwoven with humanity. It is driven by differences between one and another. While pre-agrarian societies were likely more egalitarian, the rise of concentrations of power, and thus privilege, has been occurring for many thousands of years. The Vedic caste system is an institutionalized system of privileges dating back to 1500 BCE. The many empires that arose around acquiring and protecting land and treasure were societies in which privileged royals, priests, and merchants, almost exclusively men, lived much differently than workers, peasants, and slaves.

Money and wealth is one of the most clear determinants of privilege. The more you have, the more a different set of rules apply, the more access you can buy, and the more you can get away with. Between our globalized entanglement of capitalism and our legacies of oppression and racism still alive today, it seems that privilege is here to stay.

In Alcoholics Anonymous the first step is to admit there's a problem. Accurately defining problems is an undervalued step in realizing potential. Charles Kettering, an inventor of General Motors fame, correctly stated that "a problem well stated is half solved." We, particularly those with privilege, need to get real about its presence in our lives. The problem isn't that there is privilege. The problem is that it is not being used to lift others up. If all of those with privilege used their privilege to level the playing field, the relative difference between the haves and have nots shrinks.

Self-awareness allows us to acknowledge and map our own privilege. I'm not going to hang my laundry. Suffice to say - I am privileged and I know it (said Gangham style). And the likelihood is you are too if you're reading this.

A quick note on shame here. The only way I feel shame about these privileges is if I didn't use them to benefit my fellows. I'm not ashamed of these privileges in and of themselves, most of which I was born into. It is the lot into which I am cast. My mother always said "there but for the grace of God go I" and "it's a stroke of genetic luck I wasn't born on the plains of Africa with no water, education, and healthcare." For those born into or who have accumulated privilege, the question is: *what is the responsibility of privilege?*

The primary responsibility of privilege is wielding it to expand other's access to opportunity. It is tempting to say that the responsibility is equality. Forced equality is different from equal access to opportunity. We have rarely had equality as evidenced by the millennia of hierarchical systems stemming back to earliest nomadic tribes who had hierarchical chiefdoms. Our goal is to eliminate barriers to accessing opportunity so we maintain the possibility of free will and self-determination. Ideally, access to opportunity is equal and what an individual chooses to do with that access is left to their own accord, supported by healthy parenting, whole human education, and vibrant communities.

An important question emerges. Why would someone seek to expand other's access to opportunities which if taken advantage of would seemingly reduce the relative power of their own privilege as others gain more? The answer lies in our intertwined fate.

An antidote to the many modern problems we are now facing is the evolution in understanding of humanity as a species whose common fate is total. At the species-level, we all thrive or we don't. This realization, long since emerged, now beckons us to see the complexity, interdependence, systems, and patterns that don't just link us — they bind us. By recognizing the fundamental connection between all things, expanding access to opportunity ensures all of our survival. All ships rise.

We must grow the pie but not confuse this as a raison d'être for unfettered economic growth. "Opportunity" is so quickly taken to mean the opportunity for financial well-being in the capitalistic system. This narrow view fails to account for the multiple types of capital (political, human, social, cultural, natural, built, and financial). We must take a wide view of opportunity. It is the opportunity to breathe clean air and have water. It is the opportunity to have healthy systems of education, healthcare, justice, etc... It is the opportunity to have our needs met in ways that aren't explicitly tied to money first. To have vibrant, diverse, and resilient communities.

Systemic imbalance and injustice, the hard-coded disadvantages of our systems, and the soft-coded biases in human behavior, permeate humanity. It's why the system feels rigged for so many people. It proliferates differences in access to the basic needs, most importantly education, furthering the stratification of our society. It is those who are privileged who must take the lead on tackling these issues as we are the ones who control the systems.

Sacrifice

It's amazing how much we'll give and how far we'll go for something we truly love. Have you ever marveled at the sacrifice parents will make for their children? Or the lengths that someone will go for their spouse (both healthy and not)? Or just how hard someone will work for an outcome their heart fully believes in? It seems that there are plenty of circumstances that call forth our willingness to sacrifice. We willingly give up — our time, money, or effort — and it's simply not a big deal.

There is no denying that privilege and luxury is nice-to-have. I can remember many moments in my life "being on the other side of the velvet rope", looking out from the box, table, seat, etc... on the people who weren't at that moment able to enjoy the luxury I was. I needed that then. It validated my value and affirmed my self-worth to myself. I had not yet gone on the journey of awakening, growing up, and finding true enoughness inside myself. Now I have freed myself from the games and effort required to play those games.

If you're an average American consumer, the question is: are you willing to live like most can't at the expense of others? The calculations estimate that for the whole world to live by the standard of living the USA sets as a global ideal, we would need 5.1 earth's worth of biocapacity and resources. We have to wrap our mind around the fact that we'll have to give some things up.

It's not clear what this exactly means but there are some safe bets. On the list of safe bets are reductions in vehicle ownership per household (32% of US households have two cars (including me), 22% have three or more), lowering energy usage, eliminating all single use plastics and packaging, getting off the upgrade train, and reducing meat consumption.

Why have less when you can have more? As long as our identities are tied to our stuff it will be difficult to sacrifice, en masse, even the most egregious of our unnecessary consumption like buying products on sale just because they're cheap, knick-knacks and tchotchkes, novelty decorations, cheap electronics, beauty products, fashion that won't last or you won't wear, and brand new financed cars.

The call for personal sacrifice is not a call for austerity. Austerity is a public policy that reduces expenditures with the express purpose of rightsizing public deficits to ultimately stimulate growth. Consuming less via voluntary sacrifice is about leveling the playing field between the privilege of Western consumption and the rest of the world not fortunate enough to enjoy this unsustainable standard of living.

The future requires sacrifice. It always has. That something must be given up in order for something else to be gained is a basic law of physics. We must decide what we are sacrificing to move forward. If we're moving forward with business-as-usual then we are to sacrifice a livable planet and a healthy culture and populace. If we are willing to sacrifice that which is actually not necessary for living a whole and fulfilled life, we increase our chances of having a livable environment and healthy people.

Letter: I'm Sorry, a letter to the Have Nots

To The Ones Without,

I'm writing to offer my most sincere apology for that fact that I have, and others have much more than me, and that you don't get to have as much. Call it fate, or an accident of birth, that each of us was born into our place in it all. I too have been lured by acquiring all the luxuries of modernity and continue to feel the temptation of all that is alluring and expensive. It's amazing what's available these days!

Unfortunately, the physical reality of our current predicament is that not only can we all not have more, but many of us will have to have less. What this means for you, and I get how this is unfair, is that you cannot have the whole American Dream. It was a deluded and adolescent dream anyway, natural in its arising and shrouded in a complex set of implications we are just now fully able to comprehend, perhaps too late. My hope is that you are more able to transition to the new dream that is arising, hopefully proactively and not from the ashes, the dream that transcends rugged individualism and material acquisitions and instead favors all that which stands for the continuance of life and our species. It's easier for me to hope this, having, and likely more difficult for you to receive, not having. But like children arguing over toys, it was never really about having anyway.

Perhaps we can both meet on the other side around the harvest fire, souls filled with mythic stories, hearts opened to the depth of human experience, bodies awakened to life, minds capable of holding great paradox, and egos that have matured to take their unique place amongst our human tribe. The richness of this wish, for both of us, is more than enough to make up for what is seemingly lost, for what you must sacrifice, if we are able to conceive of value beyond the prescriptions of a world we both inherited.

Thank You for Your Sacrifice,

Evan

Resources and Further Reading

- Hospicing Modernity by Vanessa Machado de Oliveira

- Sand Talk: How Indigenous Thinking Can Save the World by Tyson Yunka- porta

Twenty

Personal Responsibility and Systems Change

There's a couple episodes of South Park where there's a Latin-immigrant-hating mob that runs around screaming "they took our jobs". It's a classic example of the rabble, a viral meme that boils a larger worldview into a catchy phrase that gets people fired up. The brilliance of South Park is that their art imitates life.

The rabble cries now, "they want to take your cars, take your TVs, and tell you what you can and can't buy". The accusation is not misplaced. There are many who feel the dire urgency of the moment and will choose every opportunity to mandate and rulemake towards decarbonization, electrification, and the Green New Deal, all policy implements which require behavior change and different resource allocation.

What makes our moment different from generations past is that people were willing to sacrifice. Not just that people filled the streets in protest, but that men were willing to sacrifice their lives, women their husbands, and Americans their luxuries — all for something greater than us. "But there were drafts then and plenty of people volunteered after Sept 11" an observer could note. And yet the ethos, the feeling, was different then. There was still a belief in the myth of "the greater good". There was a fabric that held us together as a people, before vitriolic politics and vibrant every-man-for-himself-ism. We still belonged to each other in a way that inspired personal sacrifice.

It's not that your car needs to be taken away or that you need to be told what you can and can't buy. We need to unlock that same belonging to each other, the land, something greater than ourselves, that inspires the *willingness* to make a change for our children and grandchildren. Amidst the fog of war the G.I.s couldn't be sure of the outcome of the grander forces at play, nor whether they would live, but it was clear enough that action needed to be taken and it was. Though our best efforts to understand a system as complex as Earth still yields many mysteries, it is clear enough that we need to take action to reconnect, rebalance, and revitalize.

It's a bit of a Catch-22. We absolutely and completely need broad system change from the top down more than you need to start composting. If we make too much of personal responsibility we ignore the fact that people are nested in systems that shape the environment we respond to. But the systems with their sets of rules and constraints are themselves nothing more than people animating them.

The more impactful change is to reduce production first as it's the capital that's responsible for resource extraction, production, and transportation of goods and services. It's closer to the root cause. No one wants a phone or a new car until it's produced and available. Supply and demand may dictate production levels, but many companies have succeeded (and failed) with the logic of "build it and they will come".

As it frequently is with this conversation, the answer is again a Both/And. We must reduce overconsumption *and* overproduction immediately. We must take personal action reducing consumption and the demand side of the equation *and* affect broad systemic changes. We must advocate for a cultural awakening of belonging that will influence the individual *and* groups of humans whose decision-making authority can begin to reduce the production side of the equation. Chicken? Or the egg? Both!

Part Three: Coming Together

If Part Two illuminates the journey of *being* that is required to Meet the Moment, then Part Three is where we bring forth our practices of *doing*. The more one has awakened to the polycrisis and built the capacities of reconnecting, the easier the shift will be into the actions that correspond with our moment. Deeply-embodied, heart-connected, and fully-capable, we come together when we've gathered all of ourselves. It is in bringing forward the fullness of our matured capacities in commitment to service that we are able to magnetize others to rise to the occasion. As we Come Together around our moment to protect life and serve evolution we will realize our similarities, honor our differences, deepen our humanity, and expand our care. Understanding the context of our moment and engaging in the inner work is a constant and life-long process, not something we graduate from or a check-the-box. It is a living invitation to the growth and development required to successfully implement the life-affirming actions in Part Three, and the many more solutions not contained within these pages that will reveal themselves to you.

Twenty-One

Guiding Principles for Uncertain Times

S tepping outside your front door can be a marvelous experience or something you rarely think twice about as you rush on your way. To those who've attuned their nervous system to the pace of the land, the miracle of life floods the senses. Even those who live in a megacity can still feel the miracle of life teeming with an astounding vivaciousness that slows us to awe and admiration. This is feeling connected to the grass in the most manicured of subdivisions. It's having eyes that scan the concrete-and-metal-landscape for signs of an other's respiration. It's unlocking the rich somatic experience of our environment. It's the attunement to what's healthy, and what's not. It is spiritualizing the material and *feeling*, not just conceptualizing, the profound sanctity of life. It becomes easier to discern how to operate when the living world is experienced as fully alive and we reclaim our indigeneity to feel our life as one thread in the tapestry of all relations. These awakenings clarify the principles and values that create an internal framework guiding our beliefs and behaviors.

Principles and values are different. Values change over time. For example, one values sleep significantly more after having a child. You may place a high *value* on living by the water over living by mountains. Or you may place a higher *value* on having many social connections over having a few. In Part Two we considered how our values might change through the process of reconnecting to life. The set of values our society idolizes to continue business-as-usual will soon feel sorely out of balance with the livingness you more deeply feel. Values like getting ahead, looking out for your own, monetizing everything, being busy, chasing status, accepting the systems-that-be, and the many more obsessions of our adolescent culture are no longer the values needed to navigate the uncertainty ahead.

Regardless of what we value and how this changes over time, solid principles ground us to universal truths better fit for the long arc of evolution. Principles are permanent. They are closer to laws, pointing to truths we understand to be constant. For example, we hold consequence to be a principle: for every action there is a reaction, every cause an effect. As our new more life-affirming values begin to reshape our external world we must orient our actions towards a new-yet-old set of rock-solid principles to serve as our North Star:

1. **Principle of Relationality**. Are we considering all that we are in relation to? Do our actions serve the seven generations? Are we recognizing the interconnected nature of all things? Are we bringing about more harmony and balance? Does it foster an understanding and respect for the intricate web of life in which we are all a part of?

2. **Principle of Energy.** Are we stewarding, optimizing, and conserving energy well? Do we use it for good, rather than bad?

3. **Principle of Development**. Are we building our capability or that of those around us? Are we tapping into unrealized potential? Are we encouraging personal growth and learning?

4. **Principle of Wholeness**. Does it lead to greater wholeness? To the true and full expression of one's Self, the core of who we are? Are we doing the necessary internal work to meet the blocks within us that hinder our effectiveness in the world? Are we healing and wholing as is required?

5. **Principle of Regeneration**: Does it go beyond simply sustainable? Does it contribute to the regeneration of the environment and human communities? Does it lead to greater resilience and adaptability?

6. **Principle of Presence**: Are we living in the present moment with full awareness and appreciation? Does it help in cultivating a mindful approach to life and decision-making? Are we bringing about greater discernment, empathy, and compassion?

7. **Principle of Transcendence**: Are we looking beyond the immediate and the

material? Does it facilitate a sense of connection to something greater than oneself?

8. **Principle of Power:** Are we gathering power to use it well? Does it foster a sense of community and encourage collaborative efforts for the greater good?

As we come to grow our understanding of these principles we will build our capability to become a partner and co-creator with the forces of life. In doing so we are able to step into some of the highest callings that life has to offer: to be a walking blessing, to be in service to life, and to be an agent of evolution.

Prompt: Answer the questions above and consider what tweaks you might make to your daily routine and what new actions you might aspire to. Consider how you might apply these principles to a project, or even a relationship.

Twenty-Two

Self - Care

O ne cannot be a walking blessing if they can't walk. One cannot be in service to life if their own is dwindling. One cannot be an agent of evolution if their evolutionary fitness is low.

As we come into the world to action our internal beliefs we must do so from personal health. Health is our body's default state. Sickness and disease are breakdowns in that process.

Regardless of what your baseline is considering your genetic predispositions, lifelong health is a practice that requires significant effort in the modern world. Keeping ourselves healthy ensures we're showing up as our most capable selves. If the moment requires of us, it is best that we are fit to meet it. Regardless of what's coming, investing in health is singularly one of the best preparatory actions you can make for the future.

Reducing our personal exposure to the broken system of modern American allopathic medicine, with its penchant for pharmaceuticals and outrageous cost, is an outcome of our good health that reduces our contribution to the machine profiting off our public health crises. Weaning yourself off pharmaceuticals prepares you for a world where they are no longer readily available or affordable. Keeping yourself physically capable prepares you for the stresses of greater exposure to extreme elements and the physical labor required to survive them. General health increases your ability to get sick or sustain injury and bounce back more quickly. Meeting the Moment is about increasing our evolutionary fitness and personal resilience before the time arrives when it will be tested.

Self-care is a non-negotiable practice in preparing ourselves physically, mentally, emotionally, and spiritually to look, hold, and act on our moment. Self-care comprises a multitude of methods to properly care for the body and many ways to spend money on self-care, so it's important to reiterate the importance of tuning into what your body really needs, not just what you think it wants or needs. Self-care is giving ourselves what we actually need at the right time in the right way. It must always be what we need, though it may not be what we want. The practice of self-care evolves over the course of our lives as our needs change.

Our bodies are billboards for our internal world. Both scientific research and an array of spiritual concepts hold that our health is directly related to our internal beliefs. If you intend to practice the guiding principles from the last chapter in the world, first follow them with your body. Increase your *relationality* with your body, build awareness of its *energy* requirements, intentionally *develop* greater physical capability, cultivate *wholeness*, *regenerate* your injuries back to health (even your old ones), expand your *interconnection* to and *presence* with yourself and others, deepen your connection to the *transcendent* in our world. Do all of these, as described previously in Part Two and here in Part Three, and you will increase the personal *power* with which you are able to show up in the world.

With junk food at every aisle, toxins flooding our environment, and plenty of behaviors we engage in to slough off the stresses of modern life, you must make a concerted effort everyday to choose a set of behaviors that align you with your highest potential. This is a real challenge for me and in the moments when I feel myself tempted to indulge I remember that taking the right actions in the moment is dedicated to something greater than my temporary want. And when less-than-healthy actions are actually a need, I find self-compassion and make it okay. We all need a tub of mint chocolate chip ice cream from time to time. We aren't perfect.

Prompt: Complete a self-assessment of your self-care. Evaluate your current practices. Evaluate your physical self-care (diet, sleep, exercise,...), emotional self-care (expression, regulation, free time,...), mental self-care (mindfulness, meditation, goals,...), and social self-care (quality time with friends, family, and even strangers, hobbies, belonging, ...). Write a plan for the improvements you can make.

Resources and Further Reading

- Atomic Habits: An Easy & Proven Way to Build Good Habits & Break Bad Ones by James Clear, because self-care requires routine and routine is sustained through habits

- The Miracle Morning: The Not-So-Obvious Secret Guaranteed to Transform Your Life (Before 8AM) by Hal Elrod

- The Self-Care Solution: A Year of Becoming Happier, Healthier, and Fitter – One Month at a Time by Jennifer Ashton, M.D.

- The Power of Habit: Why We Do What We Do in Life and Business by Charles Duhigg

- The Body Keeps the Score: Brain, Mind, and Body in the Healing of Trauma by Bessel van der Kolk, M.D.

- Ayurveda: The Science of Self Healing: A Practical Guide by Vasant Lad

Twenty-Three

Right Doing

Buddhism's Eightfold Path provides a structured approach to achieving a wise and enlightened existence. The fourth aspect of the path is *Right Action,* which encourages us to cease harming others and actively support life through our physical deeds. The fifth aspect is *Right Livelihood* which encourages us to avoid business activities that are morally questionable. These are good models as we consider our Doing. There are a multitude of different ways to turn to the dominant systems and the people that operate those systems and demonstrate by Right Doing that with just a little imagination, some courage to step out of the mold, and a lot of elbow grease, there are novel (and old) methods of living and thriving outside the confines of the current configurations.

Each of the following are powerful technologies, models, and frameworks that organize our doing. They are possibilities, but not necessarily the right implements. It is essential that you engage in the sets of endeavors that match your place and context. Allow your proper sensemaking, Story of Place, principles, values, and expanded life connection to guide you in finding what's right for you and yours.

You will encounter new terminology in the following pages that will not be fully explained. This chapter outlines a learning journey towards powerful and clear action in the world. Read this part slowly, or make notes and come back to it, as there is a lifetime of learning in the many recommendations.

The Climate Crisis is a Food Crisis

As temperatures warm, it will be a race to see if genetically modified food, questionable in its own right, will be developed and deployed quickly enough to withstand the onslaught of extreme weather and temperatures. While the heat tolerances for many of our global staples have latitude for a warming planet, it is through the more erratic weather like late freezes, early heat, drought, and intensified hail that an entire region can lose their crop overnight. Because our food system is highly globalized, this creates enormous risk for continuing the productivity and reliability of industrial agriculture. It is essential to build greater local resilience into the food system that does not rely on grocery chains.

Permaculture is a philosophical and practical approach to land management that learns from flourishing natural ecosystems. It creates sustainable and self-sufficient agricultural systems and has been adopted successfully all over the world to work with land and create gardens that mimic the incredible complexity of otherwise untouched ecosystems. There are plenty of resources available to learn about permaculture principles and apply them in your gardening practices.

Urban Agriculture is the practice of cultivating, processing, and distributing food in or around urban areas. It enhances food security, reduces the environmental impact of food production, and strengthens community ties. There is tremendous opportunity to increase the food density of every urban and suburban area. With just a little imagination, parks, roofs, and even walls can be transformed into beautiful and productive gardens. To get started find your nearest community garden, support urban farm initiatives, find your nearest CSA, and advocate for urban agriculture-friendly policies.

Dollars are Votes

Rebalancing the economic system is the single most important life-generative systems-level shift we can engage in. It will require voluntarily changing incentive systems, methods of production, and the policy landscape to slowly redirect the tremendous cogs of production in ways that reduce ecological, developmental, and social impacts.

The Circular Economy is an economic system aimed at eliminating resource waste through reuse, sharing, repair, refurbishment, remanufacturing, and recycling. It reduces environmental impact, conserves resources, and can lead to new economic opportunities. As you develop your understanding of the inflows and outflows of consumption and waste, you begin to unlock your systems thinking in ways that will help you identify unnecessary waste and repurpose it to reduce the draw of new resources into the economic system.

The **Multi Capital Framework**, also known as the **Community Capital Framework**, is a holistic approach to assessing and reporting the broader value created by an organization. It expands beyond traditional accounting of financial capital to include various forms of capital such as natural, social, human, built, political, and cultural capital. This broader perspective is crucial as it allows organizations to evaluate their impact on all resources they utilize, not just economic ones. By incorporating wider definitions of health, including community well-being and environmental sustainability, organizations can make more informed decisions that promote long-term success and resilience inside the many systems they're nested within.

The sum of our collective individual actions can actually tip the economic scales and bring about the systemic change we need. There are a number of actions we can immediately take to begin "voting with our dollars" and thus deploy our financial capital in a way that signals our preference.

Conscious Consumption is a movement that seeks to support the companies who are taking responsibility for their ecological impact as part of their business model. Certifications like B Corporation, 2% for the Planet, Forest Sustainability Council, Fair Trade Alliance, Rainforest Alliance, LEED, and dozens of others help consumers make decisions about which products and services are the least harmful for the planet. These products are typically more expensive than their non-certified traditionally-extractive competitors and so a commitment to supporting beneficial brands without an increase in income or spending will also likely mean a lower level of consumption as well.

Local Currencies are designed to encourage spending within a specific geographic area. They help to create local economies that lead to more vibrant local business while fostering community ties and making regions more economically self-sufficient and insulated from global currency fluctuations. By using local currencies for transactions within the community, you can promote local spending and more bartering.

Relational and Interpersonal Skills

So much of Coming Together requires that we do it with one another. As such, our effectiveness is greatly regulated by our capacities to partner together successfully. We must become easier to work with so as to reduce or eliminate the unproductive squabbling, ego grabs, and misunderstandings that often cripple many promising collaborative projects.

Needs-based communication is a technique centered on empathetic understanding, collaboration, and conflict resolution. Its tremendous power lies in the listening for, understanding, and communicating our own and other's spoken and unspoken needs. This increases clarity across all relationships, and thus productivity and results.

Authentic Relating (AR) refers to a set of practices and principles aimed at fostering deeper, more meaningful connections between people through honesty, vulnerability, and empathy. It encourages participants to engage with each other in ways that reveal their true selves, beyond societal masks and superficial interactions. By facilitating genuine connections, AR helps counteract the isolation and superficiality often found in modern social interactions, build supportive communities, improve communication skills, and enhance personal growth. To get involved with AR, you can start by practicing open and honest communication in your daily interactions, seek out local or online AR games or groups, and participate in workshops or courses that teach these principles.

Read all of the following books: *The Four Agreements* by Don Miguel Ruiz, *Non-Violent Communication* by Marshall Rosenberg, *The 7 Habits of Highly Effective People* by Stephen R. Covey, *Crucial Conversations: Tools for Talking When Stakes Are High* by Kerry Patterson, Joseph Grenny, Ron McMillan, and Al Switzler, *Emotional Intelligence* by Daniel Goleman, *Boundaries: When to Say Yes, How to Say No To Take Control of Your Life* by Henry Cloud and John Townsend, *Leaders Eat Last: Why Some Teams Pull Together and Others Don't* by Simon Sinek, and *Switch: How to Change Things When Change Is Hard* by Chip Heath and Dan Heath.

Governance and Organization

Organizing people in our bioregion and community is an essential skill that requires time and effort to do well. We must seek ways of coordinating human behavior, on the most broad and micro levels, that don't involve money as the coordinating force but instead draw upon the shared sets of life-aligned values emerging from the new story.

Sociocracy is a governance system that organizes decision-making processes to ensure inclusivity and equal participation. Sociocracy is structured around self-managed circles that operate with a high degree of autonomy, linked by double connections to ensure communication and alignment across the organization. It utilizes a consent-based decision-making process, has roles filled without proposing candidates, and incorporates regular feedback mechanisms, all designed to enhance democratic participation and continuous improvement within the organization. This approach is important because it enhances organizational resilience and effectiveness by valuing and integrating diverse perspectives, leading to more sustainable and considerate outcomes.

Cynefin is a framework developed by Dave Snowden that helps leaders and organizations make decisions by categorizing problems into five domains: Simple (or Obvious), Complicated, Complex, Chaotic, and Disorder. Each domain requires different approaches for decision-making and problem-solving. By applying the Cynefin framework, organizations can contextualize their challenges, choose appropriate management and problem-solving strategies, and thereby respond more effectively to varying circumstances.

Lifestyle Changes

There are many lifestyle changes to consider that are suggested by the realities of the polycrisis and development into adulthood. How these apply to your life depend greatly on your current levels of consumption and spending. They will require both sacrifice and redirecting our personal resources towards contextually-appropriate actions.

Relocalization involves localizing our food system, economies, and support systems. Buying from local producers, and encouraging others to do so too, supports robust local economies while reducing environmental impact. Ensuring more food is sourced locally, particularly through permaculture, and urban or regenerative agriculture, is essential to reduce reliance on non-place-based supply chains. While often overlooked or under-invested in, it's important to cultivate communal, familial, and social support systems centered on meeting the needs of all.

Investing Ethically. Because the utility of money is so high, it is very easy to get sucked into profiting off of extractive capitalism. Money is a form of energy, literally and metaphysically. Where you invest it is helping to create or draw momentum from the dominators, colonizers, and extractors. There are plenty of ethical investing opportunities available now and even more coming as the world shifts to Meet the Moment and increasing sums begin to flow towards life-aligned economic activity. Principle matters.

Traveling Mindfully. If you're living a life that enables you to Meet the Moment, ideally there is less need to escape on vacation for relief from your 9 to 5. When you've connected with true purposeful work that serves life and connects you to something greater than yourself, which is what great leaders do, the propensity for adolescent coping strategies and maladaptive behavior in response to our many societal cracks disappears.

Which is not to say exploring is not fun. To travel and roam is human. But like all of our consumption, we must know why we're doing it and be mindful in pursuing it. When driving, how can you bundle more trips and errands together? Who else can come with you? When can you carpool? When flying, is the trip necessary? Are there alternative ways of meeting your needs that don't involve boarding a plane?

Rethinking Living Arrangements involves exploring alternative living arrangements like multi-generational households and co-living spaces. By reimagining how we live, we can create more sustainable, affordable, and socially supportive living environments.

The Low Tech Movement is an approach prioritizing sustainable, easy-to-use technologies that require fewer resources and are environmentally friendly. The aim is to increase ecological sustainability and personal resilience by reducing our dependence on complex, resource-intensive technologies that are often plagued by planned obsolescence. Low tech solutions enhance our ability to repair and repurpose technology while still accomplishing the necessary task. The more low-tech your tools, the greater the likelihood they will be functional if and when global supply chains deteriorate or inflation drives prices substantially higher.

***

None of these solutions are silver bullets but each in their own way will increase personal, familial, and communal resilience for future systemic shocks. They are steps to align your physical reality with life-centric values. Without action, they're not really your values, just pretty ideas you pay word homage to. As your actions align your Right Doing in the world, consider the following:

1. Not everything that looks good on paper translates well into tangible results. The juice has to be worth the squeeze.

2. Remember that you don't need to be the HBIC. Find people who are already doing what's important to you. Get a bunch of people on the phone as quickly as possible.

3. Build a crew! Get a small group of people together centered around the same goal. Have each of those people recruit one person. You've got your crew!

4. Consider your Circle of Control and how that relates to Scale. You might be fired up about a national issue, but is that the right level to assert your effort towards? Consider that neighborhood-scale is the most effective level of action and as my mother says, "become a blockhead".

5. Beware of the Valley of Disappointment, which often occurs after your initial burst of inspiration and excitement fades and you start to feel the energy lull. This will happen with many if not all projects. What ultimately determines your success is how connected you are to your values and deeper why.

"Alternatives"

There are undoubtedly hundreds if not thousands of "alternative" solutions not mentioned. Notice I put alternatives in quotes because there is something important here to recognize. Alternative according to who? The ones who are destroying our ecology for profit? Alternative to those afraid to do inner work necessary to truly grow up? The same embedded narrative occurs when referring to "alternative" health solutions. Yes, some may be fringe. But whole bodies of wisdom like Ayurveda, Yoga, acupuncture, chiropractic care, Reiki, reflexology, and Traditional Chinese and herbal medicine are labeled as "alternative" from the perspective of the medical-industrial complex. These "alternatives" have higher efficacy than Western allopathic treatments that favor pharmaceuticals and treatment over prevention. The merit of any solution is its effectiveness.

If the ideas in this chapter seem "weird", it's useful to check why. Is it because of indoctrinated beliefs, or simply familiarity with the status quo, that puts these solutions in the realm of "alternative"? To people who never lost the cultural threads of connection — primarily the indigenous in what's left in the tatters of their culture — this modern Western way of thinking about the earth, our bodies, commerce, science, knowledge, and "progress" is the "alternative" way. As it is said, history is written by the victors. So perhaps one day we'll look back from our regenerated land and communities at the gilded cage we trapped ourselves in and wonder how we allowed ourselves to be distracted by so many "alternatives" like high finance, high tech, rampant consumption, etc...

Twenty-Four

Place Based Practice

D isconnection from the living ecology of place is one of the main reasons our culture continues on as if nothing is wrong despite the flashing check engine light. Growing intimacy with place through the developmental process of maturation described in this book opens up a world of intelligence that informs our doing. None of the actionable solutions to our current crisis are possible without a deep and constant somatic, emotional, spiritual, and practical experience of one place. Your place!

We must come to know *here*. What kind of here is here? What makes it different from there? Where is the place where you know which birds come out when in the morning? Where is the place where you know the order of the birdsong at dusk? Where you know what happens when it rains, how the water runs over the land, and what directions the clouds come from at which time of year? Where is the place where you can close your eyes and *feel* the moss and dirt and grass and twigs? Where can you map the divet three leaps beyond the tall oak tree that sits just askew of the scraggly old mulberry tree the squirrels love? Where you know how the cyclical drama plays out every single season like four acts of a grand play with a majestic symphony narrating life in birth and blossom, death in drought and skirmish, color in bloom and sky, fragrance in sap and pollen, and the infinitude of other sensorial delights?

How easy it is to be a visitor in our places?! I just live here. I work there. "The scene is pretty and all but *my life is the main focus*" says the egocentric inhabitor. To inhabit is *to live in or occupy*. Occupation is the extraction relationship. This tree, park, and pond are here for my pleasure. Which means I can chop down these trees whenever I desire for my own purposes be it profit or preference.

Many people don't even notice there is a living world around them. I was walking through the beautiful and historic Westside neighborhood in Lansing, Michigan when I saw a man sitting on his front porch next to a gorgeous cedar tree. The tree had somehow grown like a miniature in that it was fully formed, and obviously old, but stood only 20 feet high. I asked him if this was his house and he said "been here 10 years". I remarked at how beautiful his tree was and put my hand on the cedar. He just looked at me and said, "what?". I said "beautiful tree!" to which he plainly responded "never really noticed...".

The played out meme of a hippie tree hugger does disservice to the reality that lies beneath those who seek to protect our trees: that we cohabit our places. To cohabit is *to live together*. We share this land. Our place is not ours nor is it a sterile movie backdrop to the set of our social media-narrated lives. It is teeming with life, an active and ever-present process that beckons our witnessing and participation.

> **Practice:** Building **relationship "ropes"** is a concept that refers to establishing and strengthening connections between individuals and the natural environment. This practice encompasses various activities and behaviors aimed at deepening one's relationship with nature, promoting greater environmental awareness, and fostering a sense of stewardship and responsibility towards natural ecosystems. These "ropes" can be built through regular engagement with nature, such as hiking, gardening, and wildlife observation. As you build deeper relationships with individual nature beings, picture the rope between your heart and the other getting larger and larger over time.

If we are to implement new economic models, old ways of tending land, and improved methods of coordinating our people and resources, it all must be in context to *here*. The coast of Maine is a different place than the Smoky Mountains, the Florida swamps, and the Texas Hill Country. The Great Lakes are different from the Great Plains, the Sonoran Desert, and the Pacific Northwest. Duh! Right?

It's easy to know that. But in your place, how well do you know that? It's easy to lose track of our unique place in a world when most ecologies are dominated by the same roads, power lines, and utility infrastructure, the same multinational companies in identical mall developments, and the same dominant economic and cultural conditions.

If you look back to the pre-colonial era there were thousands of distinct cultures with their own languages, traditions, and all the other things that make social scientists giggle. It's been estimated there were 1,000 distinct cultures in the Pre-Columbian era before western colonization of the land we know as the United States. There was no monoculture like there is today. US states and international countries span geography that used to comprise many separate cultures. These cultures arose from intimate contact with the land. It was their "here" that helped dictate the traditions of each people. And similar but distinct traditions dedicated to the seasons, fertility, life passage, etc...popped up everywhere humans cohabited.

Today we have lost those land-emergent here-based relational practices. Here has been globalized and dominated by large multinationals who standardize products and messages in order to drive efficiency and profit. The result is that Florida is much like California is much like Texas. Surely you've felt it (quit calling me Shirley!). You've traveled halfway across the country to find yourself in a scene that's practically identical to one ten minutes from your house. A gas station on one corner, a pharmacy on another, and a sea of fast food pylons poking up like a metal forest. Of course it's not true that every place is the same. But it takes some sniffing to get on the trail of Place, to get down the back alleys and back roads where monoculture and standardized building code hasn't muffled the local song of ecology.

Land loves humans in connection with it because we are the most demonstrably powerful species on it. It is amazing to marvel at our terraforming. My aren't we a destructive, er, "productive" species. And *still place calls to us*. Stand in the manicured front lawn of a cookie cutter house in a brand-spanking-new "master-planned community" where literally everything still has that new subdivision smell. Even here the land is alive, after being bulldozed and deformed, it still has a nature that makes the development in Florida different from California. Life will do its thing weaving mycelial webs, sprouting new species, and hosting new critters. It is ever seeking to create greater diversity and vitality, and despite our destructive efforts it relentlessly offers an invitation for us to be in relationship with it. Yes, even the lone tree in a wood chipped island amidst a sea of cars huddled in front of a DSW, Sephora, and Michael's still invites you to its shade, the microcolony of ants crawling up its bark, and the texture of its leaves. Beneath the overlay of concrete is place, alive and longing for our recognition and relation. Yes, we have the power to pave and erect. We also have the power to save and respect.

A place is both one we choose and one that chooses us. As our relationship deepens we realize the symbiotic nature of our cohabitation. It requires us to move slowly. Nature can be skittish. She's moving on an infinitely longer timeline than our lives and yet will also share many of her patterns and secrets with us if we slow just enough to pay attention. You don't become best friends instantly. Maybe quickly, but relationships always take time to develop. It's important to recognize that most places have a lot of history with our species before we showed up. There's both a personal relationship and a species-level relationship and it's important to understand both. To do that, we must know the Story of Place.

Practice: The Story of Place

Embark on a learning journey about your Place. This will take some time. Track your learnings somewhere. Here are some prompts to get you going:

1. What are the geologic processes that took millions of years to create and shape your place? What happened before and after the last ice age?

2. What might the land have been like just prior to modern humans?

3. Who were the first people native to the land? What was their culture? How did they live?

4. Who were the first settlers/colonizers? When? Why?

5. What is the arc of population and progress from that time?

6. How has modernity precipitated a set of ecological, cultural, economic, and social issues?

7. Find elders, people over 80 years old, and go talk to them.

Use your skill of pattern tracking and follow your intuition as you sense in this Story of Place. Research alone cannot yield a full picture. Take your new knowledge out on the land. Go to the places where events may have occurred or where you feel connected with the past you've learned about. Sit with your place. Ask it to share its story. Listen. Open yourself to receiving its nature. Listen.

Why bother? Imagine how all of your actions may be informed by your most intimate understanding of Place....

The future is Place Based, Bioregional, and Hyperlocal.

Bioregionalism

Bioregionalism is not a new concept but it has gained more significance as a place-based movement capable of shifting how we physically structure and care for earth. It is centered around bioregions, areas that are defined not by arbitrary state and national boundaries on the map but by natural boundaries like rivers, lakes, forests, soil type, and more. The purpose is to bring together the places that share a similar topography like Cascadia in the Pacific Northwest, the Sonoran Desert in the Southwest, or the Great Lakes. These bioregions are not just bound by physical and environmental features. One of their most important characteristics is their shared culture, emphasizing local history, language, knowledge, and solutions.

Bioregionalism is a way of organizing humans that brings us into closer contact with the land, its rhythms, and requirement for care. It emphasizes sustainable practices that ensure long-term environmental vitality, localism, and the consumption of local goods. Through local initiatives that emerge from the ground up, literally, rather than national edicts from the top-down, the bioregionalist perspective challenges the monoculture of global consumer culture, replacing it with rich, vibrant locally-sourced food, materials, and culture. While aimed at restoring and preserving local ecosystems and promoting local food production and consumption, this approach's true achievement is realized in the deep cultural intimacy with nature that brings harmony between human living and the natural world.

The features and constraints of a particular bioregion become the most important elements in the thoughtful design of lifestyles, economies, and governance structures. Using the skill of systems thinking, bioregionalists endeavor to map the intricacies of their watersheds, geology, flora, fauna, and human activity to reveal the many patterns of place that differentiate here from anywhere else.

Bioregionalism seeks to devolve power from artificial structures such as states and reconnect our membership identity back to the geophysical realities of our world. Each of us at this very moment are in a bioregion that has its own unique resources, character, and potential. Centering this understanding is essential to building community resilience from the ground up and ushering in more human settlements harmonized with the planet. It is a vision that moves us beyond consumption into deep stewardship, inviting us to govern ourselves in ways that are just, democratic, and considerate of ecological health, the common good, and the seven generations.

Regenerative Design

Bioregionalism works parallel to the ideas of Regenerative Design which is a body of practice that seeks to restore natural systems by designing human projects that bring forward the unique qualities of each particular place. Influenced heavily by the philosopher Gurjieff, regenerative design as a movement has calcified on a set of principles and practices that encourage us to develop a Story of Place, understand the true essence of it, map the flows and patterns of a place across time, and vision in a way that taps into the latent potential, the possibility that already exists but does not currently.

Regenerative thought leaders Bill Reed, Daniel Christian Wahl, and Carol Sanford have offered the seven principles of regeneration as the keys to the holistic thinking required if we are to regenerate our places, people, and culture back to health at the same time. Writer Ernesto van Peborgh summarizes the principles as:

Wholeness: Whole Systems Thinking

- Holistic Integration: Advocates for a comprehensive view, integrating ecological, social, cultural, and physical aspects.

- Interconnectivity and Synergy: Emphasizes the interconnected nature of ecosystems, ensuring harmonious relationships between all elements.

- Resilience Through Diversity: Focuses on the diversity within systems to build resilience and adaptability.

Developmental Approach

- Continuous Evolution: Promotes adaptive strategies for ongoing evolution in dynamic systems.

- Capacity Building: Aims to enhance the capacity and capability of both human and ecological components.

Essence

- Unique Identity and Character: Recognizes and honors the intrinsic qualities and unique character of a location.

- Authentic Expression: Ensures design solutions are reflective of the unique 'essence' and story of the place.

Potential

- Unlocking Latent Opportunities: Identifies and nurtures the inherent potential within ecosystems.

- Empowering Innovation and Creativity: Creates environments for individuals and communities to express their potential.

Reciprocity

- Mutual Benefit and Relationships: Establishes balanced relationships based on mutual benefit and cooperation.

- Building Collaborative Networks: Encourages collaborative and supportive relationships among community members.

Nodal

- Strategic Engagement: Identifies and engages with critical junctures within the system where significant interactions occur.

- Holistic Impact: Recognizes that interventions at nodal points can influence the entire system.

Nestedness

- Interconnected Hierarchies: Acknowledges the complex hierarchy of relationships within systems.

- Holistic Transformations: Focuses on systemic changes, recognizing that interventions at any level can impact the entire nested hierarchy.

This framework is an invitation to moving beyond the linear, reductionist models of intervention. It encourages us to consider the perspectives of others, what is called external considering. In doing so, regenerative design is a powerful practice that shows us *how* we can move beyond our ego and human-centric paradigms to embrace the complexity and dynamicity of living systems. If we are to work with nature to increase its vibrancy and sustain our living we must begin to think in new ways with new metaphors that help us to think like nature itself.

Resources and Further Reading

- Regenerative Development and Design: A Framework for Evolving Sustainability by Regenesis Group

- The works of Carol Sandford

- Permaculture: A Designers' Manual by Bill Mollison

- LifePlace: Bioregional Thought and Practice by Robert Thayer

- The Design Pathway for Regenerating Earth by Joe Brewer

Twenty-Five

After Growth

"Growth for the sake of growth is the ideology of a cancer cell."

Edward Abbey

M any have pointed out that infinite growth on a finite planet is an equation that simply doesn't pencil out. And yet our economy is predicated on this very math. If the economy produces 100 widgets this year, it must create that same 100 plus three more next year. Despite this modest 3% growth, at this rate an economy will *double* in just 24 years. It's difficult to wrap one's mind around double the cars, double the materials, double the candy bars, clothes hangers, cell phones, underwear, books, scented candles — double *everything*. Economists will be quick to point out that mature, industrialized societies are transitioning to services-based economies, which, while true, belies the fact that all money ties back to energy and a loan taken from the future. This does not lighten the load on our ecology.

The assumption that we have to grow is just that, an assumption. There are groups of people who have seen the challenges of the polycrisis and are working out how to simultaneously reverse growth while maintaining well-being and ensuring a more just distribution of economic activity across the globe, particularly in the Global South. These groups largely coalesce as a movement called Degrowth. Degrowth is an economic, political, and social movement that advocates for the reduction of a nation's economy with the aim of achieving environmental sustainability and social equity. It challenges the traditional focus on economic growth as a primary objective of economic policy. The concept of degrowth emphasizes the need to decrease the use of natural resources, reduce environmental degradation, and improve the quality of life through non-consumptive means like building community, increasing leisure time, and promoting local economies.

Degrowth proponents argue that continuous economic growth is unsustainable in a world with finite resources and that it often leads to environmental destruction, increased inequality, and a decline in the quality of human life. Instead of measuring success through gross domestic product (GDP) or other economic indicators, the degrowth movement suggests using alternative measures of well-being and sustainability. The degrowth strategy includes a range of proposals that can be measured, such as reducing working hours, enhancing public transportation, implementing policies to redistribute wealth more equitably, and it often directs much of its focus towards the highly developed world.

Many bemoan the societal and ecological effects of capitalism declaring that "capitalism has failed." On the contrary, if the goal is to expand commerce and capital across the globe and create enormous wealth, capitalism has been a wildly successful experiment. As we consider the realities of inequality, systemic fragility, and overshoot:

we must declare a new experiment
that optimizes for a different set of goals.

Critics of degrowth note that it will send us back to the stone ages, which is a reasonable concern for any Westerner nestled in their high-tech convenience. They also accuse proponents of degrowth of supporting authoritarianism, that moving in the direction of slowing down the economy will require totalitarian-like control, sometimes described as ecofascism, to force into austerity everyone who believes in their limitless right to do whatever they want. They charge that for economies built on the assumption of growth it would not be feasible to slow down as it would create a slew of socio-economic challenges. These critiques have merit. Change has always been hard. The shift to the economy we have now did not occur without massive struggle. This struggle still occurs, though it's largely removed from Western eyes by design.

Wrestling control of the system from the hands who currently benefit from the status quo will require widespread political, civil, and social action. It will not be comfortable for anyone. Anticipating this, the winners at the very top of our current system are fortifying the many systems that will keep their hegemony in place. Considering the massive advantage the 1% has over the 99%, it would take true adults to sacrifice such privilege. Only humans fully connected to life would slow the gargantuan cogs of industrial progress and courage the repercussive ripple effects that would inevitably have to be dealt with. The chances of this voluntary distribution of power are slim. Whether entitled by blood, fate, God, worth, or merit, our industrialists and tech oligarchs have every personal adolescent incentive to reinforce the current system.

We forget that all of this has been an experiment. Capitalism is an experimental reality tied to political philosophers of the 18th and 19th centuries. Democracy is no different. Yet we've stopped experimenting. It's as if we tasted the fourth Baskin Robbins ice cream flavor and declared the other 27 flavors uninteresting without trying them. The last constitutional amendment was ratified in 1992 and most of our economic, fiscal, and monetary policy is designed to keep the perpetual growth machine running with low inflation and full employment.

Despite the immensity of what we've built on top of this system we must summon the courage to continue experimenting and steer civilization in new directions, rather than simply deeper down our current path. By necessity degrowth will require sacrifice as we right size production, reduce overconsumption, and reallocate resources within planetary limits. Shifting the economic paradigm will not be so scary if we've gone on the journey to find wholeness.

Resources and Further Reading

- Less is More: How Degrowth Will Save the World by Jason Hickel

- Slow Down: The Degrowth Manifesto by Kohei Sato

- The Future is Degrowth: A Guide to a World Beyond Capitalism by Matthias Schmelzer, Andrea Vetter and Aaron Vansintjan

- CASSE (Center for the Advancement of the Steady State Economy)

Twenty-Six

Paddling Upstream

When you fully grasp the precarity of our moment to the point that you begin to make tangible changes in your life, you will almost certainly run into doubts within yourself and plenty of external resistance. The status quo and business-as-usual has such momentum and near-total pervasiveness that it's totally reasonable to question whether or not you've lost the thread.

People will laugh at the sacrifices you begin to make for possibilities that do not seem imminent to those not giving Right Attention. People you love and who love you might be the ones to laugh. You will see people with their shiny new toys and feel foolish for abstaining from the consumption addiction. First mover advantage will make you feel silly. It will seem like you're falling behind. Like the whole world is on the hedonic escalator and you're going the wrong way. The Joneses will pass you on the gameboard of Life. The temptation to turn around and go back to the seemingly safe cocoon of modernity will be constant. You will feel the FUD lurking (fear, uncertainty, and doubt) and wonder whether it's you that has gone mad, or the world.

As my friend Snake says, "capitalism is a fucker". Around every turn you will encounter the cold, brutal reality of capitalism clawing at your pocket book. Your willingness to engage in the system as it's constructed, in the manner in which you always have, will likely change and with it your cash flow. Not much stimulates concerns about safety and well-being as quickly as the money conversation. As you feel the pulse of what's alive through your ecological enmeshment in the network of life, the option set of how you're willing to invest your precious life energy will change. It will feel maddening that what suddenly feels most valuable is least paid and what is least valuable is most paid.

You'll long to go back to before you knew. You'll wax romantic about ignorance being bliss. You'll flirt with just pretending that everything will be fine. You'll wonder why you're paddling so hard upstream. Wouldn't it just be easier to go with the flow? Two day shipping sure is convenient. Around every corner the system will invite you back, ask for your money to get out of it, or downright block your exit.

Why choose the hard path? There's always another point of no return down the road, right? Maybe the next generation can take care of it. You can always turn around. And you'll be welcomed with arms wide open back into the mass hypnosis. Paddling upstream is hard. It requires *a lot* of effort. Particularly when those closest to you are not evolving towards Meeting the Moment.

But then you'll remember there is more than one current. The economic-and-cultural-current is heading downstream towards glamor, largesse, and the inherent risks of modernity. You'll remember that the power of this current, of capital, is overwhelming and relentless yet it is not more powerful than the current of life.

You'll tap into the reality that the general current of modernity, with its economics, politics, and culture, is the force that is moving upstream powered by 500 billion invisible fossil fuel workers. You'll feel the current of life heading the other direction, downstream, and when attuned to its flow it will guide you to wholeness, health, and vitality.

Tides go the other direction. They come in and they go out. Just as sure as cannabis consumption was illegal one year, recreational use is now legal. Things in human culture fall in and out of favor. Each of us has a part in helping to shape the culture as a small voice amongst the fray that is saying, "hey, this is the right way". Upstream may take work, but that upstream is only against the predominant culture that will inevitably shift, either by choice or by necessity. Voluntary adaptation is going to be a lot easier than involuntary adaptation. All of the action that is required, from advancing one's internal capabilities to building personal physical resilience, is made easier when connected with the current of life.

Paddling upstream against our dominant culture requires a spirit of resistance and exploration. The most effective activism is changing your behaviors, redesigning your life, and engaging others in the internal and external work of Meeting the Moment. This will not come without substantial resistance. It's important to realize that most people were not taught to deeply question the merits of the system around them. They've had decades inside the system and the more it works for them the more they seemingly have to lose. They are scared by your suggestions and/or demonstration of a different way to approach living. These people are used to everything in their life being so consistent and reliable that they've forgotten this is not the way it's always been.

Do not be surprised when your ideas and choices are challenged. Expect that those still operating from the dominant egocentric growth-fixated paradigm will seek to deny and discredit you in an attempt to keep their worldview, identity, and trappings safe. In these moments when the tension arises between what you're choosing to live and what's uncomfortable for them, it's important to "hug your haters", to look through the eyes of compassion, not take it personally when they resist your conclusions or explorations. Keep in mind the developmental lens and consider "how do I Meet the Moment of their fear or long-programmed beliefs?" Hold space for them to disagree, perhaps vehemently, while never wavering from the realization of what you're in service to: life.

As evolutionary agents, provocateurs on behalf of a healthy future, we must be sensitive to where each person is on their journey. This is no small leap we're making. It challenges the safety and assumptions of a civilization building its dominance for three centuries. That it is difficult is to be expected. This is a tall order, one that is both aspirational and necessary. Despite the urgency of our moment, we must not force the resistant. Rather than push, we must become a gravity and through our healthy selves and aligned actions become strange attractors that pull others toward the work in this book.

We're Not Alone

Against what can feel like an unrelenting tide of brainwashed masses happily chugging their way over the cliff, it's important to remember that we're not alone. Strike up a conversation with a stranger on a bus, at the grocery store, or in a bar, and chances are you'll be able to find a significant amount of agreement, lamenting even, about the challenges that face us. What's particularly interesting is having these conversations with people who "sit on the opposite side of the aisle". You will inevitably discover that with many (but certainly not all) there is a common set of identified challenges and what's really different is how the challenges are addressed.

Better yet, talk to a lobbyist or civil servant, even a first-term congressperson and each will likely acknowledge the naivete of their early aspirations for service (regardless of who or what they're serving) and the many limitations of both the system and coordinating humans.

Claiming our personal sovereignty and agency means that we will not sit around and expect our life to become resilient by work of the state or some other actor. That's the opposite of taking responsibility for our lives. The reality is that while probably everyone sees some cracks, many won't admit them and prefer to ignore them. And for all those cracks that are seen, unadmitted, and ignored, there are still a tremendous amount of people who are working on them. In building a values-aligned business in climate tech, I spent dozens of hours researching groups and startups to support. The task opened up my aperture to take in the vast scale and scope of everyone who has seen some tiny little crack of the monstrous fissure and devoted their precious life energy to that one piece. As we paddle upstream, we can do so with our hearts full of the knowing that so many others are giving their one precious life to bring about solutions to the polycrisis.

My place, your place, is filled with people doing the work, who are earnestly upleveling their internal and external skills to Meet the Moment. We are not alone. Voluntary adaptation, place-based solutions, and adult sacrificing are on the rise. The momentum of solutions-oriented doing in the world will only increase the more our moment comes into view. This is evolution itself acting through each of us.

And this is a team sport. As monkeys, we were never meant to go it alone. The social nature of our species locks in our deep desire to do this with Community. We are not meant to grieve all that we've lost and are losing alone. We are not designed to uplevel our sensemaking skills alone. We are not designed to experience an ecoawakening without the whole village being ready to support the task. And all of the systems and practices that ground us back to the source of life require that we do it together.

Henry David Thoreau wrote that "the mass of men are destined to live lives of quiet desperation." Remember that there are so many people in the same boat. They feel the quiet desperation of the system as it's been designed, the drudgery of modern work, the reliance on retail therapy, the shakiness of the cracks closing in, and the deep freedom their heart longs for. These are the same people who showed up to the Occupy Wall Street marches. The same people who show up for Earth Day and climate protests. These are many of the people who voted for Donald Trump because they feel the blatant disenfranchisement of a system that failed them.

Practice: Talk with a "stranger" about our moment, prompt a certain question, and see how many people actually feel the same disillusionment when you really get down to the truth. Use the context of where you are to broach the topic.

- Talk about prices if you're at a point of sale. Chum the waters with something that's easily overlooked while waiting at the grocery store.

- Food |" I'm so grateful for this meal. Have you ever thought about the complexity of the system that brings all of these ingredients from around the world in order to make this meal possible?"

- Gas Station Pump | "It's amazing to think that our entire civilization has been built because we have this liquid gold, eh?"

But don't stop at disillusionment, create an opening to talk about the new story. Shift the conversation towards what you know is possible.

What inevitably you'll discover is that many people share some of your same beliefs. No, not all of your beliefs. But some. Enough to find common ground. Particularly if you can listen in the conversation for what someone is really saying, their real concern beneath the meme they're repeating.

Whether you embark in the world to find common ground with people inside your circle of concern/influence or not, trust that *you're not alone.*

Twenty-Seven

From Me to We

Part of not being alone is understanding that we can't do it all ourselves even if we tried. But this is not The American Way. It's not the Western Way. Unlike the traditional cultures of the Global South and the Orient, Western culture has the longest love affair with Individualism. In our culture we believe whole-heartedly in a single person's capability to accomplish. Our myths and our lore tells tales of the individual overcome. We laud overnight successes and relentless persistence. We triumph natural born talent and cultivate growth mindsets to develop mastery through the 10,000 hours. Magazines and TV angle the biopic and millions chase their moment in the spotlight. Everyone wants to make it but even better if it looks like *I made i*t. It wasn't until the time of the enlightenment that we began to single out individuals as the source of genius. Before that time we thought people had genius, not were genius. Now with an internet megaphone the appearance of genius and mastery are too often crafted by clever marketing and a good bio with headshot.

The West is built on Rugged Individualism and it is glorified in the United States. It's the myth that holds promise of our personal genius, the lure of 40 acres and a mule, the promise of the next gold rush. Anyone can build a new empire with the right combination of elbow grease and a little luck. "The world is your oyster", "it's ripe for the picking", "there's a fool born every minute" – all aphorisms in common vernacular that we perpetuate as little meme-stories propping up our love affair with individuality. At the end of the day it matters much less how you put up the points but that they're there. So much is done inside the meme that life is about "survival of the fittest" where fitness in our culture is defined as your propensity for self-serving behavior and willingness to step on others to get ahead. Yea, "it's a dog eat dog world out there" they say. Economic Darwinism validates that those with more money are more fit and thus we have created a system whose incentives are to get the money through any means with no shame felt for the person we have to be in the process.

The self-centeredness of this whole worldview is alarmingly familiar to me. I used to prescribe to this mindset as I schemed my next million-dollar idea that would "take advantage" of ripe market trends. The fiber of this way of being is extractive at its core, focused on what you can do for me, what I can do for me, such that my financial wealth and relative advantage increases. Of course this isn't everyone, but it sure is hard not to "play the game", to paddle downstream because it comes with increasing luxury that is pretty enjoyable.

There's nothing inherently wrong with this orientation other than the fact that it goes against nature. Surplus rarely exists in nature. Efficient systems ensure that any amassed surplus is effectively distributed. Fortune does not last for long in nature. Healthy ecosystems are marked by high levels of exchange, strong and interconnected flows, and high genetic variability. In them many different types of species are able to acquire the sustenance they require. What would happen if a certain species started hogging all the water? Or another species started gorging itself on the total available food supply? It would throw off the whole dynamic balance of the life system. This of course does happen in the micro and the ecosystem balances one way and another. But it's a far cry from the Western environment of unfettered free-market capitalism which drives cut throat competition at the expense of the planet and communities of living beings.

Consider the downstream effects of all of your actions.

As we survey our personal actions it's important to investigate all of the downstream effects of those actions. "Hey, I didn't decide the rules of the game". No, you didn't. Yet playing the game is a way of supporting it. What type of world do you create when you vie for this or that? What sets of behavioral norms do you reinforce when you play the game? How does unhealthy focus on Self eventually harm the Other?

May these be the old ways, according to the new story, the story that affirms the reemergence of a New Communalism, a centering again of us in the way we go about our lives. This is an entirely new cultural value set for the west, yet one less foreign to the many cultures whose collectivist ethos has not yet been fully erased by the western ideals of individualism and capital. This shift back, from Me to We, readjusts the centerpiece of our attention from ourselves to our community and the broader field of life in which we are intimately enmeshed. Faith-based communities already model and live this well.

> **Prompt:** In a world where we idolize billionaires, how do we tell the story that rugged individualism has failed? What new story is emerging that recontextualizes individual achievement from the perspective of a greater community of human-and-more-than-human beings?

I am not suggesting that we turn Western democracies toward communism. Our greatest possibility is a world in which we maintain a high degree of individual sovereignty and through our maturation from adolescence to adulthood voluntarily opt for the many outcomes that a collectivist society would choose for itself in the context of our current moment. This is emergent cooperation from the bottoms-up, bioregional and hyperlocal governance, community resilience efforts, more equitable economic models, and the plenitude of other actions that must not be forced by a centralized government that isn't here, familiar with our Place.

Community and Connection

Isolation is both a feature and a bug of modern culture. Every week an article declares that there is an epidemic of loneliness in the United States. Social media provides a facsimile of healthy social relationships. Political polarization works hard to demonize and push the other side away. Our lives are busier than ever leaving less time for friends and family. As it dragged on the Covid-19 pandemic exacerbated an epidemic of loneliness that was already occurring as people became more siloed and migrated more of our social interactions from in-the-flesh to digital.

What we have been losing for decades is vibrant, healthy community. Community is the social architecture that we as humans have relied upon throughout our history. We rely on community to bring connection, deep relationships, social and physical resilience, and ideally a group centered around meeting the needs of the one and the many.

Our journey to community must first start with our belonging to the community of more-than-human beings that share our place with us. It is essential that we develop a reciprocal, mythic, and sensuous relationship with the land. It is this fragrance, an embodied knowing of the relational web of life, that can be the biggest gift to our human communities. We must be emissaries on behalf of all life working to expose as many people as possible to the realities of our moment and the great heartbeat of life that connects us all and bids us to protect it.

There are many communities available to us: civic, church, school, hobby, etc... Most exist within the dominant cultural paradigm celebrating growth, encouraging distraction, or ignoring our challenges all together. Of course a running club or a biker group isn't oriented around Meeting the Moment. And it's important that we have places we can go for respite or simply the enjoyment of life that makes all of our efforts worthwhile. But this must not come at the expense of having a soul-initiated, polycrisis-aware community committed to taking individual and group responsibility. When you're part of a group of humans who are tapped into the rhythms of nature aligning their communal living with the palpitations of the seasons, much as our grandparents and great-grandparents did, there is a distinct feeling of wholeness that fills the heart and motivates the types of actions that enhance connection with people and place. Unfortunately this is not an experience that many people know for there are too few people who have crossed the threshold into true adulthood.

In traditional communal living our proximity to others is closer than in modernity. Modern cities provide a distinct challenge as many people live geographically dispersed from one another. Polls show that people are less neighborly now because of the loneliness factor, loss of social skills, a mentality of retreat, a focus on entertainment, increased commuting time, and general busy-ness. We're less likely to meet our neighbors and the people we do gather with are likely to live farther from us. It's a perfect recipe for isolation, rather than an environment conducive to building a life-oriented community.

The more you travel the more you realize how similar human motivations are across languages and cultures. Generally we all want the same things, our needs are in fact universal, it is only the details of what that looks like that varies. As much as we believe we're different, and we are, we are more the same than we want to admit — a fact that is difficult to reconcile for many of us who have grown up with the spirit of individualism. The better our community helps to fulfill these basic universal needs we all have, the healthier and more fulfilled we will be.

There are a few collapse-aware communities that are taking active steps to build individual and communal resilience besides many of the intentional communities which are focused on spiritual well-being or a retreat from, rather than a meeting of, the moment.

I have found and am constantly finding tribe through a trial-and-error process and as my evolutionary journey continues to evolve. There is a tribe out there for you. Unfortunately you may have to search for it or build it. In a perfect world, it'd be the people who you live closest to. Most are still plugged into the matrix. Your opportunity is to be a living invitation to awakening and a demonstration in your very being of how to live a soulful life. Some will notice, others will inquire, and those that are ready might come along.

If you are an agent of anything, be an agent of disruption. Come alive in a manner that effuses all that is true, beautiful, and worthy. Allow the totality of your living to be permeated by the greatness of life you're connected to. Demonstrate your strong NO and your clear YES aligned to the values that serve the seven generations and human evolution. Show up and listen with your whole body. Be a strange attractor, a humble magnetic force that pulls others in by the merits of your soul, the wholing work you've done, and the maturation with which you now move.

Be a living invitation.

Find your tribe and remember, we don't all get along. This is expected. People have different beliefs and preferences. A healthy forest has a variety of trees at different heights of the canopy and a healthy community has a spread of different ages and stages of life. In nature, diversity breeds resilience. The greater the diversity of a garden or a forest the greater the ability for it to absorb and recover from a shock. It's important that as we build community we work towards diversity, however that is defined, so that we all benefit from a variety of perspectives that aids our sensemaking and keeps us from the peril of groupthink.

We must develop tolerance, interest, and curiosity about other belief systems and ideas. We have a dearth of this in our society right now, but having done the necessary ego work, one can easily engage with, sensemake, and even strawman other people's beliefs without it threatening their own, or even have their own perspective shifted if they are open to really seeing and receiving the value of other's ideas. It is in the layer of deep understanding that we begin to comprehend where someone is along their developmental path and how best to invite them to Meet the Moment.

Seek first to understand.

There are many books about community and likely many people who are actively building community in yours. Building community is easier than you think if you put in the time and the effort. You must be persistent over time in putting yourself out there. Be vocal about who you are, what you believe, and what you desire. You will get what you want by asking for it and by making your intentions known. Speak to your why, your understanding of the world, what you dream of, what you're on behalf of, and engage others from your wholeness. The right people always show up in the long-term because we're wired for community and it may be more important now than ever as an answer to the many dynamics of modernity.

More and more people are waking up to the dangers of our time. I find this in how pervasive many of the topics of this book are in the daily conversations I'm able to have with a broad range of people. The complexity of the polycrisis' hydra-head is showing itself in many places and awareness is growing. Against great powers of industry, media, and technology, greater numbers of our neighbors are coming to the conclusion that through solidarity with each other we have the greatest chance to Meet the Moment. We do our work for them, for the living breathing ecology of place, ourselves, and for our progeny.

Intentional Community and Co-Living

Okay, we got it Evan. You're a freaking hippie. Move to a commune already. We don't use that word anymore? O right, now we say "intentional community". You should move to one. Maybe. If only it were that simple.

People have been going back to the land for a long, long time. There's a reason the trend keeps emerging across the last 125 years. As each successive wave of innovation occurs and society lurches into the next age via another industrial revolution, there are a small group of people who realize the trade-offs are not necessarily worth it. Eventually some number of these people wind up at the conclusion that moving back to the land facilitates a more wholesome and balanced way of living.

It'd be a shame to sum this book up as "yep, move back to the land". As much as that seems romantic, it's not feasible. It's not a feasible outcome yet because the internal growth required to make it possible hasn't occurred amongst a broad enough swath of society to make it a true movement. Moving back to the land might be the outcome of the process of eco-awakening but it does not solve overshoot by itself.

Our opportunity is to Meet the Moment of where our global society is, increasingly urban or suburban, disconnected from nature, and removed from the physical methods of providing self-sufficiency. While deurbanization seems likely as we derisk population density and resource draws, the reality is that we cannot simply move onto the land. Rural prices will skyrocket in the current economic system becoming another privilege for the economic winners; this is already occurring. But the bigger concern is that we don't have the built environment to support a reverse population migration from our major urban metropoli to the more spacious countryside. We have spent many decades investing our physical resources in the built environments of suburban and urban living. There's no quick fix, no undo switch, even *if* the mass of people are willing to give up the convenience, variety, and excitement of the city.

As a movement, intentional communities and co-living arrangements appear to be a step in the right direction. Intentional Communities are defined by the Foundation for Intentional Community as a group of people who have chosen to live together with a common purpose, working cooperatively to create a lifestyle that reflects their shared core values. By living communally, connection is higher, more physical and emotional needs are met, and footprint is lower. Co-living is a broader movement that includes intentional communities as well as more transitory housing like co-ops.

The challenge is that one must sacrifice some personal space. This is a problem because humans are annoying. Fascinating, yes. Sometimes quite lovely, yes. And also just a pain in the ass. Irrational, moody, and complex. The benefit of our single-family (house/apartment) living is that others outside our family unit are not exposed to our neuroses. Inside the comfort of our walls we don't have to work for it. We don't have to try as hard to lean towards our best selves. We are not forced to develop the requisite skills to actually *live* with other people. We live near other people, but just far enough removed that we can act and decorate like we want.

Co-living, just like the increasing popularity of non-monogamous relationships, requires us to develop emotional regulation, communication, and needs awareness skills. The reality is that the closer we live to other humans the more likely we are to have conflict centering on a difference of needs and wants. When people gush about the evolution of consciousness, the place where the rubber meets the road is in the sets of intra-and-inter-personal skills required for effective relating. These are the byproducts of an elevation in our being that improves how we communicate, the flexibility we find for difference, and the discernment between need and want.

In theory long-term co-living comes with a host of benefits including:

- reduced consumption, increased sustainability, and better cost efficiency

- deeper relationships, a built-in social network, and a sense of community leading to reduced loneliness and greater cultural exchange

- personal learning and growth opportunities as one navigates the complexities of living in close proximity with other humans and all the messiness that naturally entails

We trade these benefits for the luxury of every house on a block having their own lawnmower, microwave, big screen TV — their own everything — so much of which sits idle most of the time. Our need for sanctuary is just another outcome of the dysregulated world we occupy, where trading time, health, safety, or contentment for money requires recovery strategies that look like buying more stuff, vegging out on entertainment, scrolling social media, or any other of the multitude of ways we seek to numb ourselves to the hidden cost of modernity inside the confines of our own space.

Living close to other people requires time. Building relationships, trust, and mapping people's idiosyncrasies takes effort. And who's got the time for that? The egocentric mindset wonders what the payoff is for learning someone else or, god forbid, putting up with their shit. Lest we forget we've all got it.

Self-deception is one of the most tricky inner games we play with ourselves. At the moment when our disconnection is greatest and nature is far, we have tricked ourselves into lifestyles that lead us away from more connection, particularly the deep and intimate human-to-human connection that plies at our heart, inviting us to risk being vulnerable. The type of connection that dwarfs conversation about the latest reality show season or last night's sports game, not that these topics don't serve their purpose, but in the urgency of this moment in time, with lives literally on the line, we need the type of connection that places ourselves in service to that which is greater, other, and within us.

Twenty-Eight

Life Design

There are so many ways to live and so many choices available to answer Mary Oliver's famous question, "what will you do with your one wild and precious life?" There is no "right way to do it" despite how vehemently others will advocate for or sell you on their particular prescription for living a good life. This book is no different in that regard.

And yet there does seem to be a particular script that is generally followed. You know the bit. Go to school, get a job or start a business, buy a house with a mortgage, get a couple cars in the driveway, have kids, build multiple streams of income, take vacations, get a second house, save for retirement, invest in your hobbies and all the stuff that comes with them, work your way up the ladder, etc... This "life on automatic" works well enough because it does address many of the core human desires for purpose, safety, and belonging.

In life there is more than one path to the same destination. We can discover purpose, feel safety and belonging, and get our needs met without fully opting into the hungry beast of capitalism. It is essential to engage in Life Design that is nestled in the context of our moment. Life Design is a careful consideration of your true needs, as determined by your whole Self, combined with the courage to imagine different ways of meeting those needs that might fall outside of "the standard script".

The standard script is safe. Its well-beaten path, complete with healthcare and a 401(k), is reliable enough for most. It takes courage to step away. From my own personal experience, and from observation, I fully get just how difficult it is to make the leap. It took me, and others I know well, months or years to summon the courage to move beyond scarcity fears and the need for a perfect plan. "I'll never have enough money saved up" say people with both $10,000 in the bank and $1 million. "I don't know what I'll do. How will it work?" All the questions and fears pop up, which the more inner work you've done, the easier they'll be to allay.

And once on "the other side", after making the leap, how exactly do you design a life that allows you to align your living, and livelihood, with your understanding of what's true about our moment? How do you begin to change your behaviors and take actions that advocate for individual, communal, and systems change? Here are some design considerations:

- **Take the next right step**. From the outset it's not entirely clear how it will all play out. Outside the script the plan is a bit (or a lot) fuzzier. It will ask you to find your courage, confidence, and faith. It will require your deep listening, tuning into the subtle threads of your own nature and the raucous fray of the world. You won't have it all figured out, but then again did you *really* have it all figured out for yourself on the standard path anyway? Remember, you're not going alone. Eat one bite at a time. Poet David Whyte says:

  Start close in,
  don't take the second step
  or the third,
  start with the first
  thing
  close in,
  the step
  you don't want to take.

- **Get comfortable with "The Pathless Path"**. In his book of the same title Paul Milliard encourages readers to embrace uncertainty and forge individual paths that align more closely with personal values and inner fulfillment, rather than adhering strictly to societal expectations. He suggests that true contentment comes from creating one's own unique journey.

- **Optimize for Time**. It is truly our most precious resource. For all intents and purposes, money is unlimited. But we are only given so many days of our life. How precious are our moments? How much potential remains ungerminated in underutilized time? Would you be willing to have less trappings and more leisure? Would you give up your 24/7 connection to social media or your work email for more real human connection?

• **Rightsize your balance sheet.** Go after your debt like a dog chases squirrels. Debt is modern slavery in that it often traps us into doing things we otherwise probably wouldn't do in order to afford the payments for things we might not need. Reports suggest that 25% of Americans go into debt to pay for their basic needs, a fact that is inexcusable in such a rich nation but which also points to the fact that 75% of debt is spent on non-essential consumerism. Whatever your debt afforded you, do you really need it? Or that much of it? Do you need a 3,000 square foot home? Maybe if you have ten children. Do you? Do you need a Mercedes SUV when a used Toyota is more efficient? Rightsizing your lifestyle is essential in making the leap. As long as you're aiming at some arbitrary accumulation, like a luxury car or a really big house or a life complete with all the latest clothes or gadgets, you will never be free. In the immortal words of rapper The Notorious B.I.G. "more money more problems". The fewer your needs, the less you'll be required to do to meet them. And then the more time you can invest in yourself, community, family, and service.

Do you need all those monthly subscriptions? How might you repurpose that time or money spent eating out and on entertainment? Not to demonize eating out or entertainment, I'm going to a concert tonight (cost: $25). But how often do you spend on such things? You need less than you think you need. I canceled my Amazon Prime, Netflix, and several other subscriptions months ago. Remember that marketers spend billions of dollars each year to convince you of your needs and even invent entirely new ones. You will be amazed at how many life-affirming endeavors you can fill that time with!

• **Wait for big purchases.** If there's something you desire that you know is probably not essential, wait on it. Wait longer than seems reasonable and gauge your level of sustained interest over time. If this is a purchase you continually desire and you've searched the reasons for it, eventually it's time to make the purchase. The delayed gratification will make the experience of whatever it is that much sweeter. And the initial hesitation will keep you from unnecessary splurge purchases.

• **Reclaim Rhythm.** Nature moves in rhythm and cycles. Developing sets of practices that align to the cycles of the moon and seasons are important in reorienting ourselves back to nature. Consider gathering, fasting, or dancing on the new or full moon. Celebrate the solstices.

Designing a new life that wrestles with the typical modern constraints and reimagines how needs can be met is an incredible journey and exploration in itself. It will take you to novel places with neat people and challenging, life-affirming work. It's led me to volunteer with nonprofits working on urban eco-restoration, build a business in climate tech, and proliferate a global network of heart-aligned individuals each Meeting the Moment in their own way.

Are you willing to risk the future health of our planet, of our species, and the soul of our culture so you can follow the wide superhighway of the standard path to comfort, ease, and abundance? Or are you willing to risk discomfort, challenge, and the fuzziness of being on a less defined path to be a part of the commendable evolutionary force propelling us towards a livable, healthy, and viable future?

Question Everything

Why do we do stick-built housing construction? Why has the cost of housing gotten so expensive? Why is coliving not more popular? Why do we take on more debt to buy a new car or new phone when the old was perfectly fine? Why is the food system like it is?

It seems that so many of us accept the way things are without questioning them. We forget that we made it all up. That all of the human world, everything we've built, every rule, law, and system we've installed, that somewhere in a not too distant past a person or group of persons made a decision, likely optimizing for a set of private interests rather than the true public good, and now that's the way things are.

Question everything. Why? Why? Why? Why? Why?

Relentlessly seeking to understand the "why behind the what" of our world is a way of taking what seems nailed down and loosening the boards a bit to see what's underneath. By those that study intelligence, in particular the many types of intelligence beyond what is measured in a standard IQ test, it has been suggested that curiosity is a more important trait than raw intelligence. Dubbed the curiosity quotient (CQ), it is the level to which we seek new knowledge and novel perspectives. One hallmark of curiosity is the tendency to not accept the given assumptions and instead question the context directly. There is immense power in the right questions and grave danger in the wrong ones.

How else might we tease out the tradeoffs of progress? How else might we follow the trail of acorns into the forest? How else might we come to question the hungry ghosts of capitalism? How else might we unravel the layers of numbness to truly come alive?

So much of our world is accepted by assumption. Systems and processes work because that's the way they are. Things will never change because they haven't. Curiosity is the relentless vine of inspection, ever searching for a crack to open up.

Imagination & Willpower

"You cannot solve a problem with the same mind that created it."

Albert Einstein

When considering practices like place-based regeneration, reducing consumption, and coliving, it is imagination that affords us the possibility of reaching into the realm of potential to vision solutions to our current predicaments. Imaginal thinking is one of our species' greatest capabilities. Paradoxically it is also one of our greatest threats. It all depends on where we point our imagination and what we serve.

Directed towards personal gain, profit, and "progress", imagination can dream of bulldozers with wheels bigger than your house and machines that can pick up an entire tree and strip it of all its branches in one seamless motion. It can dream of derivative trading markets, get-rich-quick schemes, war profiteering, and endless shopping mall parking lots. When imagination serves the self, we miss out on the best chance to dream a new future.

When imagination is tapped into the rich fertile landscape of serving life, meeting needs, and partnering with evolution, we unlock transformative new realities. In the imaginal realm exists the new myths which seek to have their story told. We don't have a lack of imagination. The charlatans of decades past have dreamed detailed schematics of utopias. Ambitious ideas exist for most challenges we face. Perhaps there actually was a water-powered automotive engine. Perhaps Tesla did have plans to tap unlimited free energy.

Endless rows of cookie-cutter suburbia are not a lack of imagination, they're optimizing space and return-on-invested-capital. Our "justice" system isn't a lack of imagination, it's a profit center and ideological showcase. Our education system isn't a lack of imagination, it's a semi-productive machine creating obedient workers and higher education debt. In these and practically every other societal element we have plenty of worthwhile reformations that would serve the humans inside these systems.

Imagination dies somewhere up the line where "the math just doesn't pencil out". Imagination dies in the hands of those who lack *will*. Without will nothing gets done. With it we can move mountains, literally and figuratively. Will is our desire for change and our drive to make it so. It is undetterable will that has led to excellence and mastery, to revolutionary breakthroughs, and our greatest works of art. It is will that has built empires and destroyed them or amassed fortunes to squander or secure them. It is will that makes us willing to sacrifice today for tomorrow, that finishes homework, and motivates tired parents. Without will nothing happens.

Will can be mustered, found, falter, or rally. Will itself does not set the direction but determines if and how far in a direction we'll go. Will is an indispensable partner to our Being. Determined will from a hateful being and you get the Holocaust. Determined will from a loving being and you get the nonviolence of MLK, Gandhi, and Mandela. Will can change the world, a lack of it and it can change for the worse.

> "The only thing necessary for the triumph of evil is for good men to do nothing."
>
> Edmund Burke

Right now, lurking in the imaginal realm, is some idea, a seedling of potential that you at the most fundamental nature of your essence are supremely qualified to make manifest. Perhaps it's an idea that's visiting many of us at the same time, calling forth our evolutionary allies who we will build and reform with together. Ideas whose time has come. Ideas which are older than any of us. Imaginings whose threads disappear into the mythic tapestry of what it means to be human. Possibilities that scare all of those safely ensconced in the security of "that's just the way it is." Latent potential begging for your curiosity. Inventions that optimize for all the types of capital. New systems that regenerate life and create more equity. Ways of relating that increase tolerance and enhance liberty. And an untold hidden iceberg of solutions that will reconcile tensions.

Capturing these imaginal wonderings, like a floater in the air, is the easy part. As if doing the work to redirect the imagination away from self-only and towards the whole-including-self is barely a lift. Then we must come together, as communities once raised barns, boosting will to support each other in making the bold, daring, and cunning dreams we dare to dream a reality.

Resources and Further Reading

- Pathless Path by Paul Milliard

- The works of David Whyte

- The works of Mary Oliver

Twenty-Nine

Leverage Point: Education

O f all the individual crises that comprise the larger polycrisis, education has the greatest long-term potential because you have to get them when they're young. McDonalds understood this and thus the Happy Meal was born. The urgency of our moment means we cannot wait 10 to 15 years for children to work their way through the educational system. We can't just kick the can to the next generation; we need action now. Yet our both/and thinking requires of us that we also invest heavily in education reform. Doing so will have a greater impact than any other public investment.

The true leverage point is the economic system and how every other crisis dovetails with it. But as I've set out to extrapolate in this writing, we must do the inner work to make the bold, hard, courageous choices necessary for reimagining economics and redeploying its limbs. The most critical action we can take is to redesign our education system and raise *an entire generation* of humans who are immediately proficient at Meeting the Moment because we designed an early life that gave them the necessary skills us older folk must retroactively develop. We must reform our education system so that it prioritizes:

- building intra-personal skills like cultivating greater self-awareness, somatic intelligence, emotional resilience, and sensemaking

- building interpersonal skills like effective communication, needs-awareness, leadership, and tolerance

- systems thinking to increase understanding of the interconnectedness of the modern and natural worlds and build deeper literacy of complexity and energy

- critical thinking so that we have a generation that constantly tests the critical assumptions of our world and seeks to evolve them

- nature connection so that a common culture of care for and intimacy with nature expands

This agenda is not "woke". Any set of political or religious beliefs can exist alongside it. It represents a focus on fostering the necessary faculties required to be better citizens and neighbors. It optimizes more for revolutionizing the current system than for fitting into it and will empower a generation of children to grow into wiser, more equipped adults than we currently produce.

Children are our future. It's pithy, cliche, and true. In the absence of broad adjustments to our educational curriculum the responsibility to equip our children with these modes of being, thinking, and doing will fall to our communities and their ability to support parents in raising true adults. It takes a village, the more close-knit the better, one filled with soul-initiated adults in right relationship with nature, elders who pass on wisdom and life-affirming myths, and teachers who impart the skills required for children to grow into both.

Resources and Further Reading

- Education in a Time Between Worlds: Essays on the Future of Schools, Technology, and Society by Zachary Stein

Thirty

Reconciliation

G lobal politics has become hyper polarized as the inevitable result of our sensation online world that exploits our attention to drive ad revenue. The divide between left and right has never been bigger, more fractured, or more contentious than it is now. Most politics is identity politics, us vs them, exclusionary, based on a particular identity, such as race, nationality, religion, gender, sexual orientation, or social class. Demagogues and ideologues on both sides of the aisle use inflammatory rhetoric to make everything about identity. You're either with us or against us. Dysfunction is the strong preference to compromise.

Amidst the gridlock of polarization and downright demonization of neighbors and fellow citizens, a return to the founder's original intent of Federalism is the most practical approach for Meeting the Moment. The United States was originally conceived by the founders, and is enshrined in the Constitution, as a confederation of states. Certain rights were reserved to the federal government according to the 10th amendment and all others are reserved for the states. Over the course of the last 250 years the executive branch of government has continued to exert greater control and influence over the governance of our nation. Whether through the Interstate Commerce Clause, by executive order, or instructed by Congress, the executive branch has ballooned into the behemoth we have today, a sprawling network of departments and agencies with incredible budgets and intersection with our lives. Big Government indeed.

The right, paternalistic, lambasts government overreach but is happy to force its morals on you while the left, maternalistic, clamors for the state to take a greater role. The two sides are locked in an ideological battle that traces itself back to the origination of democracy and contentious debates between the early political philosophers. That you lean one way or another is the result of your upbringing, socialization, preferences, sensibilities, and experience. And as long as you define your views along a spectrum between two poles, "left" and "right", you like everyone else will be stuck in a polarity.

A polarity by definition is a tension for which there is no resolution. Both sides believe they are correct and there will always be a valid case for the opposition. The constant factious fighting is doing little to bring compromise. The reality is that, just like co-living with other people, coordinating groups of people is hard. If you've ever planned an event or led a group of people in one capacity or another you know this. It's unlikely that the founders could have predicted their political experiment would grow to encompass the land mass it does, a population of 330 million people, an economy (and debt) this large, or our geopolitical position in the world today.

If our future is to be place-based then it must emerge from Place. A government in Washington DC cannot best sense and respond to the intimate needs on the ground. We must reconnect the governance of our places back to the land. Our current politics is hurtling toward the future energy blind, denying collapse, locked in the left-right-polarity-doom-loop, and servant to classical economics and the capitalist machine.

A new political philosophy is needed that ushers in a new wave of federalism and devolves power back down from the centralized institutions of national and global power. Local resilience and vibrant local economies will not happen when we are overly reliant on the federal government. As we learn to trust and bolster the quality of emergence, as thoughtfully guided by soul-initiated and mature cultures, we can begin to unwind Big Government and reconnect governance and coordination to the people most connected to Place.

This political philosophy must prioritize Liberty. We should be free to do what we want as long as my freedom doesn't impinge on yours. Do what we want in our bedrooms, with who we want. Free to love who we want. Free to identify how we choose. Free to have as many guns as we want but not free to use them on others, obviously. Free to abort babies. Free to do meth or mushrooms. None of these things impinge on anyone else's right to choose, or not choose them. That their existence is morally repugnant to some and not others is an issue of the personal development required to be a citizen. It is a minimum entry fee to freedom. You can't have it one way and not the other. Don't like abortion, don't get one. Don't like guns, don't buy them. Don't like drugs, don't do them. That people who have different preferences are in your awareness and that makes you uncomfortable? That's your work. Grow up.

As more and more people awaken to the ecological crisis, proactively through engaging in the work or reactively as the more palpable and personal effects of the polycrisis are felt, a new political movement must quickly emerge that reconciles many of the tensions of the past in ultimate service to stewardship and bioregionalism. No longer "is the world flat", as Thomas Friedman famously wrote in the book of that name which coincided with the expansion of a hyperconnected global economy.

The structures of globalization that shape our socio-economic reality are shifting under our feet, laying bare the systemic fragility of the supply chains that make Western living possible. Even as we reorient to smaller, more local living, our global interconnectedness requires that this new political movement occurs simultaneously across the globe for several reasons. First, ecology is not local. Air pollution and rising temperatures have no concept of country boundaries. Our highly-linked global economy, and the unlikelihood of us unwinding it, means that the entire human species does in fact share the same outcome. No people will be spared our collective fate. Second, the dynamics of rivalrous geopolitics make it difficult to be the first state actor to begin backing away from the perils and plunder of the global economy. Paradoxically, the sooner developed countries do so, the more they will be able to prepare for the challenges ahead. How this is done in a manner that doesn't jeopardize state security is a greater issue for the rest of the world which shares continents and does not, like the United States, enjoy the natural barriers of oceans, extreme levels of militarization, and the most well-armed populace in the world.

As if calling for a global ecological political reformation is not grandiose enough, this also must occur without the brutal forcing hand of authoritarianism, totalitarianism, and fascism. Tops-down one-size-fits-all solutions are unlikely to be the answer as they are out of context with local places, people, and culture. We must also not place all of our hope in a single leader, or be swept in by the cult of personality, both of which breed fragility. Our rotation must be away from polarization and towards unification. We need robust, emergent bottoms-up leadership to spring up like mushrooms from the mycelial underlayer of life's pulse. To the degree that tops-down mandates are required for broad systemic change, *in an ideal world* these policy decisions will reflect the broader revolution of emerging ecological consciousness which places a greater value on the biosphere and its beings. These two must move independently given the urgency of our time, but in parallel, with many people realizing the necessity of reduced economic consumption and lifestyle shifts before they've been mandated. Laws and legislation should lag our cultural (r)evolution.

Building consensus across the centuries-old battle lines of traditional and progressive political thought will require sacrifice. There is a future that, when reasonably considered with the higher ideals of life in mind, should pacify many of the tensions. If we are to evolve we must take the best of our previous stages of development and the ideologies that have dominated our past, combining them with reemergent life-oriented beliefs into a new political movement that carries us forward into the future.

Thirty-One

Stop Taking This So Fucking Seriously

Nap Activism

In a world that seeks to capture all of your data, monetize all of your attention, and optimize all of your behavior and translate it into profit, the most radical action may simply be taking a nap. Refusing to run as hamster on wheel, the deliberate act of slowing down as a purposeful antidote to the great rush around us is a rebellion against much of what our world has become. It's quite a delight to lean back and watch the headlines zing on by, to miss the news of the hour, to watch the madness roar.

> **Prompt:** Go somewhere where there are lots of people on the move. Perhaps a place to sit and watch the traffic, or a busy mall (if those still exist). Watch the humans scurry about and marvel at how busy it can seem. Imagine the cell signals bouncing back and forth and the bills that were paid to clothe, transport, and educate these people. Watch long past you normally would until you fully feel the rush around you in contrast to your full idleness.

Today one of the biggest protests to a world gone haywire is to just...STOP. To dedicate time to listening to the river and the trees and the birds. To watch the grass grow or a plant gesture towards the sun throughout the day.

It's paradoxical that, at this time of great urgency when all heads, hands, and hearts are needed, perhaps the most important action to take is no action. Not as in doing nothing or continuing on with business as usual, the inaction that blindly ignores the stakes of the moment. The inaction that is purposefully doing nothing at all but slowing down, waiting, and watching. A retreat of stillness that doesn't require booking an idyllic airbnb. A pause that doesn't require any preparation.

Just...stopping.

Taking a nap at 10:30 in the morning. And again at 2pm. Daring to spend time where not only are you not getting ahead, you're getting nowhere in particular.

To the world that demands more, less is a daring protest. Doing less. Buying less. Having less. The silence of rest and the stillness of pause, if you can arrange to actually experience them, are a declaration of your willingness to say, "I know there's a different way". Sometimes taking a nap can be the biggest protest. The future needs you well rested anyway.

No...seriously!

If you're like me, or even kind of like me, you have the tendency to carry the weight of the world on your shoulders. I'm compelled to not look away. To witness the grotesqueries of our individual and collective actions. To invest time researching and musing over how we got here, why, and how we get our fingers out of this confounding finger trap. To consider which bite of the elephant is mine?

At the dark end this veers towards doomerism, hopeless day terrors that all is already lost. It flirts with misanthropic ideas about the long-demonstrated-and-little-changed reality of human nature. It surrenders to the memes that "all is lost" and the Four Horsemen of Personal Responsibility. It throws hands toward god, goes gambling, orders a double, goes on a two-day delivery shopping spree, and tears up the mall with the belligerence of a person who has nothing left to live for.

It's easy to take all of this SO seriously. Because the truth is that it is serious. In fact the stakes are higher than any one person can hold or carry. Our mental health matters. And this whole reality is not our making. Nor will we solve it alone.

There is a middle way between completely ignoring the problem and the all-consuming-ever-present-and-depressing weight of the polycrisis. This middle way is the practice of the "Yes, And". As in, "Yes as I take in all the data the future looks bleak, *and* I realize that both hope and inaction will not suffice." "Yes there is much to lament, *and* I know this shows me how much I actually care for." "Yes I know the power of business-as-usual is immense and my Circles of Control and Influence are comparably small, *and* I will take action because it's the right thing to do."

And perhaps most importantly: Yes, and despite all of this, *I'm still going to stop and smell the roses.* I'm still going to create beautiful art, make beautiful love, and seek to luxuriate in what's still left of the tremendous natural beauty of the world.

"If you take life too seriously you'll never make it out" is but another cliche for a reason. Amidst all the work this journey calls for, through all the hard truth-telling and reworking of programmed patterns, in the sacrifice, and with all the effort needed from each of us, we must also have fun.

If we're not having fun, we're doing it wrong

There must be time for playfulness and relaxation of the kind that increases our connection with what all of this is for. We must find the amusement parks of the decadent forest, endlessly scroll the deep intrigues of our in-the-flesh relationships, and search the timeline of canyons and sediment layers.

As we cruise toward our inexorable future, the human ship having devoured all other ships, let us make love to life anyway. Let us make love to what's left of the wild, singing praises, writing poetry, and getting lost without a watch in the bosom that sustains us.

Let us realize the absurdity of it all and laugh at ourselves. Let's feel secure enough to mock our own sacred cows, to find the truth in satire, and the wisdom in sarcasm. Let us chuckle at our own importance, cackle at the latest GDP report, and harangue ourselves at the memes we see in action.

Let us afford ourselves compassion when we break down and make an impulse buy, you know the kind that's advertised on Instagram. Or when the pressure of it all, or just our little daily stress, has us waste a half-tank of gas driving nowhere in particular.

Let us remember that perfect is the enemy of good. That action taken today from a good heart and pure will is infinitely better than no action taken yesterday. That whatever we do next will be a bit sloppy. The first take probably won't be pretty. That we can still celebrate our imperfection. That it is human to err.

Let us remember that we got in this together and the only way out is together too. So best make it a party, where we celebrate all those who continue to arrive in deep, connected relationship. Let us make uproarious welcome every time someone moves from ego to eco.

Let us forget all of this and get lost in the eyes of our lover. Let us tell the children of our dreams for the future, our imaginal flirtations of all that is possible in the hope we still dare to nurture.

Let us stop on an empty patch of ground, listen to the dirt, nurture it back to soil, then plant roses just so we can stop and smell them, pick one, and give it to that person we care about just for them to smell that smell for a brief moment before the petals fall dead onto the table in the ultimate symbol of the ephemeralness of life — and still feel all the effort was worth it.

Better yet, let us toil in the ground for a regenerated forest whose speckled shade we will never sit in and still be fueled to work day after day by the knowing in our bones of the vibrancy of that future ecosystem teeming with life.

Let us become masters in the art of embodying paradox, simultaneously reckoning with the seriousness of our time while moving in a manner that tells of our taking it lightly, and of our joyousness for all that is good, true, and beautiful.

As we continue to up level our personal aptitude for healing, wholing, communicating, relating, sensemaking, and holding nuance, it's my experience and hope that we will continue to see our world in ways that orient us away from disconnection and dis-ease and towards being, doing, and a value system that is more life-centric. Much will fall away. Much will emerge. May we be proactive, rather than reactive. And have fun doing it!

Thirty-Two

How to Meet the Moment

Practical Actions to Take

This list is hardly revolutionary, plenty have belabored these points in depth. My hope is that having ventured into the personal journey towards Meeting the Moment that the HOW and WHY of bringing yourself to these actions is more clear. This is your call to:

1. Embark on the journey of self-discovery and inner transformation, *because being before doing.*

2. Hone strong competency at one barterable skill that would have been useful before the invention of the computer chip, *because technology is not a guarantee.*

3. Grow food, *because the climate crisis is a food crisis.*

4. Become energy aware and reduce your personal consumption, *because less is more.*

5. Actively seek and build community, *because we must do this together.*

6. Consume mindfully, buy quality, and take a stand against disposable consumption, *because your choices matter.*

7. Reestablish your intimate connection with nature, *because it is our birthright and responsibility.*

8. Find beauty everywhere along the journey, laugh, play, and create, *because life is worth living.*

9. Titrate your attention, *because there are forces seeking to knock you off track.*

10. Build Habits, shrink the change, and make the big small, *because actions become habits which become your life and your impact.*

11. Anchor your why often, write it on your mirror, and talk about it more, *because the going will get tough.*

12. Remember that the process itself is the reward, *because embarking upon these actions is a destination itself.*

> **Prompt:** As this book comes to an end, it's time to create an **Intention Sheet.** Sit with the many different topics we've covered in this book and consider what's most alive for you. Develop a plan for two or three immediate internal and external actions you will commit to yourself.

As we arrange ourselves and our society we must orient towards that which brings more beauty, life, and well-being. Not the fragile well-being of adolescence that needs things or status to prop up its worth. The deeply-rooted ecologically-connected service-oriented well-being of maturity that fills its cup from the communal fountain of life. The high stakes of our urgent moment invite us to take radical, not incremental action. This is not the time for half-measures or name-sake platitudes that make for strong headlines but weak change. We must increase our capacity for voluntary discomfort. The courage required to do so will not be found inside modern comforts.

There's the grand global moment we share. And then there are all the moments of our lives. To truly Meet the Moment, we must be present for what our life is personally asking of us. Our opportunity is to understand what it means to bring our whole selves to each and every moment. Who do we have to be to rise to the occasion? Which of our many capabilities are required? And how might we humbly sharpen our skills to better Meet the Moment? Even the most innocuous ones like going into the grocery store or eating lunch with coworkers are opportunities for us to orient towards the maximum possibility of the moment. What of our being and doing will bring the most life to now? The most connection? The biggest challenge? And how do we anchor this developmental worldview across daily life?

How to Get Lost Along the Way

It is easy to get lost along the way. It's much harder to stay the course amidst a world that will do everything to tempt you to veer towards indulgence, pleasure, and distraction. And if the world doesn't knock us off track, our complex personal world of programmed inner protectors is likely to try and self-sabotage our path.

Some getting lost is good. Getting lost in the woods, on a wander, or away from the scripted path of success can have enormous benefits. This getting lost is not just beneficial, it is likely essential in distancing oneself from the status quo world of business-as-usual. It isn't really getting lost but you'll only understand that in hindsight. In this getting lost, there is a feeling that where you are and what you're doing is right enough, and it also comes with a sense that this stop is temporary and will likely change.

Then there's getting lost in the way that you've allowed yourself to revert back to old protective strategies, become distracted or numb, or have fallen into a trap along the way. Here are some common traps to watch for:

- **Focusing too much on healing**. Yes it's beneficial, *and* too much medicine becomes bad medicine. Discern how much healing is enough to get you back moving with momentum towards Meeting the Moment.

- **Falling into Consumerism**, which is so easy to do because starting a homestead requires *a lot of stuff*, as does equipping oneself for wilderness excursions to facilitate eco-awakening. Be mindful about consumption, look to buy used or borrow gear, and when purchasing buy quality so resale value is higher and you're likely to have the item for a longer time.

- **You're overworking**, which is easy to do when you're fired up about some-thing, yet it's important to remember that vitality is the goal of the new game. The longer you can keep playing the game the better so ensure you are getting enough rest.

- **Or you're resting too much**, which can happen when you're working too much, holding the weight of the world on your shoulders, or just avoiding facing reality. Seek to find a dynamic equilibrium between work and rest, ensuring you're getting enough of both.

- **You're not learning or perfecting new skills,** which indicates that you may have plateaued, which unless for the purposes of rest, is a sign to reconnect to your why and reapply yourself to skills that align with the vision of what you're building toward. Ideally your development occurs in a progression that is visible and designable by you.

- **You've become insufferable**, which is understandable because once you've done the research and you really see what appears to be true about the many existential risks we face, it's hard to look away or stop talking about it. Life is extraordinary and must be worth living in its beauty, joy, and love if we are to fight for it. Take a breath, go for a walk, get dirty, eat some ice cream, look at some art, watch the sunset, dance, read a good book. Whatever you do, remember to be a living invitation and consider who you have to be to attract the people you want to make this new story a reality with.

Thirty-Three

Getting Involved

There is no shortage of action to take. You have inner work to do. And outer choices to make. Where to start? I invite readers to check out this book's companion book *Meeting the Moment: A Spoken Word Poetry Collection*.

As you journey forward each day, may you be open to the many mysterious processes that are seeking to express themselves through you. May you lean into co-creating with the beings of the land, your ancestors and descendants, and the forces of life that know what the true nature of your essence is. May you find the courage and the compassion to Meet the Moment in ways that align your Great Becoming with stories and myths worth telling. And may you say yes to getting lost, just enough that it helps you orient back to what really matters. Remember, the way knows the way.

Afterword

Parts of this book read quite naively. The likelihood that those with the most to lose will go on this journey of inner-and-outer discovery seems slim. Yet all of my sensemaking winds back up in the same place: *we must do the inner work if our external world is to change.* The presence of logical, viable, just, and executable solutions is simply not enough.

There is a world of reasons to not do the inner work. Crossing the chasm becomes more and more difficult under the mounting pressures of modernity. Being on the other side, ingratiated with life, you discover the kind of solidity of knowing and being that is required to stand firm against the cultural flood (literal and figural) eroding our relationship to life. As belonging emerges, a cornucopia of behavioral changes bloom to reveal our care, capacity, connection, and unique contribution. We find that doing the hard things becomes easier for us even as the challenge of the task at hand remains the same. We know what must be done. Many choices are no longer available to us and new ones reveal themselves with a previously unfelt clarity. Whispers from the wind give us confirmation. Mystery unleashes synchronicity. And soon we find ourselves in the flow of life, downstream, fully animated and alive with free will and yet perfectly a part of nature's orchestra. Our listening informs us. Our senses guide us. Our awakened bodies help us navigate and operate with greater effectiveness.

I have seen enough of the process in myself and others to know that it is entirely possible for many of us. But it will not happen by accident or default in our current culture. Across the world there is a resurgence of interest in the pagan, mythic, and indigenous ways of being. This is no mistake. It is an evolutionary response to the toxicity of modernity that is swelling rapidly in the collective conscious and springing up within each of us. The more we open ourselves to these evolutionary threads the more quickly we'll begin to arrest control of this behemoth called Modernity and steer it towards pro-social, life-generative, and culturally healthy destinations.

We have much work to do if we are to Meet the Moment. May we all find ourselves in relation to that which is greater than us and the courage to act for it today.

Appendix 1

NATURE CONNECTION EXERCISES

- **Nature Journaling**: Spend time observing nature and document your thoughts, feelings, and observations in a journal.

- **Sit Spot**: Find a quiet place in nature to sit regularly, observe the surroundings, and notice changes over time.

- **Tree Hugging**: Hug a tree to feel its energy and connection to the earth, and to ground yourself.

- **Bird Watching**: Observe birds in their natural habitat, noting their behaviors, calls, and interactions.

- **Nature Meditation**: Meditate outdoors, focusing on the sounds, smells, and sights of the natural environment.

- **Grounding**: Stand or walk barefoot on natural surfaces like grass, sand, or soil to connect with the earth's energy.

- **Forest Bathing**: Spend time in a forest, immersing yourself in the atmosphere and allowing nature to rejuvenate you.

- **Nature Art**: Create art using natural materials like leaves, stones, and twigs, or draw/paint natural scenes.

- **Cloud Watching**: Lie on your back and watch the clouds, letting your mind relax and wander.

- **Stargazing**: Spend time looking at the night sky, observing stars, planets, and constellations.

- **Wildflower Identification**: Learn to identify wildflowers in your area and document your findings.

- **Nature Photography**: Take photos of natural scenes, plants, animals, and landscapes to appreciate their beauty.

- **Gardening**: Engage in gardening to connect with the soil, plants, and the process of growth and nurturing.

- **Animal Tracking**: Learn to identify and follow animal tracks, observing the signs of wildlife presence.

- **Nature Storytelling**: Create and share stories inspired by nature, either real experiences or imaginative tales.

- **Beachcombing**: Walk along the beach collecting shells, stones, and other treasures washed ashore.

- **Building a Shelter**: Use natural materials to build a small, temporary shelter, engaging with the environment creatively.

- **Seasonal Observations**: Observe and document the changes in nature across different seasons, noting how plants, animals, and landscapes transform.

Appendix 2

LOGICAL FALLACIES

Logical Fallacy	Description	How It Applies to Overshoot	How to Address the Bias
Ad Hominem	Attacking the person making an argument rather than the argument itself.	Discrediting scientists or activists based on unrelated personal attributes instead of addressing their evidence on ecological limits.	Focus on the arguments and evidence presented, rather than the characteristics of the individuals presenting them.
Straw Man	Misrepresenting someone's argument to make it easier to attack.	Simplifying or misrepresenting arguments about ecological limits to make them appear flawed or easily refutable.	Accurately represent opponents' arguments before refuting them, to ensure the debate is grounded in what is actually being argued.
Appeal to Authority	Claiming that because an authority thinks something, it must therefore be true.	Citing the opinions of non-experts on ecological issues as if they were definitive evidence.	Evaluate the relevance and expertise of the authority being cited in relation to ecological science.
False Dilemma	Presenting two options as the only possibilities, when in fact more possibilities exist.	Framing the response to ecological overshoot as a choice between economic growth and environmental protection, ignoring sustainable dev options.	Acknowledge the complexity of ecological issues and consider a range of possible actions and outcomes.
Slippery Slope	Asserting that a relatively small first step will inevitably lead to a chain of related events culminating in some significant impact.	Arguing that any attempt to address ecological overshoot will lead to extreme measures, such as economic collapse or loss of freedoms.	Assess claims critically, considering the evidence for each step in the argument rather than assuming an inevitable conclusion.
Hasty Generalization	Making a rushed conclusion without considering all of the variables.	Drawing broad conclusions about ecological overshoot from a single event or a limited set of data points.	Look for evidence from a variety of sources and consider the broader context rather than basing conclusions on isolated incidents.
Appeal to Ignorance	Asserting that a proposition is true because it has not yet been proven false, or vice versa.	Claiming that because ecological overshoot cannot be disproven, it must not be happening, or conversely, that lack of evidence against overshoot proves it's happening.	Require proof of claims made about ecological overshoot, recognizing that the burden of proof lies with the person making the assertion.

About the author

Evan Carr is an author, spoken word poet, entrepreneur, and creator. He believes that art and culture are the most important instruments for us to Meet the Moment. He dedicates his life to human development and the many ways we're called to act in these important times. He currently lives in Denver, Colorado where he dances, explores nature, and rapturously loves the world.

Evan recently released a poetic companion to this book titled *Meeting the Moment: A Spoken Word Poetry Collection*, which is an invitation to consider the challenges of our world and the journey we might go on in response through the prism of poetic though. He is the co-founder of GoodRev which accelerates companies that are good for the planet and people by capitalizing and bringing their climate tech to market. He is the creator of Loveable, a first-of-its-kind social wellness app that transforms your phone into a broadcast device for love and goodwill. He is the creator of OffsetAI.earth, a platform to helps organizations measure, report, and offset the environmental impact of their AI usage. He invites you to email him at mtm@evanbcarr.com

Made in the USA
Middletown, DE
25 November 2025

22099399R00119